W9-CBR-090

Praise for
Inside the Leader's Mind

'I believe in leadership books that offer practical advice. *Inside the Leader's Mind* achieves this in three ways. It allows aspiring leaders to share the real experiences of successful CEOs and chairmen and women. It also raises awareness of the issues that new leaders will face, and it's always better to go into new situations with your eyes wide open. And finally, and most importantly, it offers real advice on how to build your own authenticity as a leader. This book doesn't tell you how to be like someone else, who is already a famous leader. It helps you to become a skilled and authentic leader in your own right. For me, this ranks alongside Goffee and Jones' book *Why Should Anyone Be Led by You?* in its capacity to offer helpful guidance to leaders.'

Ian Powell, Chairman and Senior Partner, PricewaterhouseCoopers, UK

'At blackswan, we believe in business transformation through innovation. This fresh look at how a leader thinks hits squarely into our own belief system. Unless business leaders are comfortable with the uncertainty and risk taking that underpin successful innovation, nothing changes. *Inside the Leader's Mind* addresses this head on. These five ways of thinking like a leader are so obvious it is a wonder someone hasn't thought of them before. Follow this advice and you will become a better leader.'

Maurice Duffy, CEO, blackswan

'Leadership matters in all walks of life, from companies to NGOs to nations. It makes a difference. For me, the most important message in *Inside the Leader's Mind* is that leaders need a solid core; a reserve of instinct, experience and integrity that lead them to do the right thing.'

Phumzile Mlambo-Ngcuka, Former Deputy President of South Africa

Inside the leader's mind

FT Prentice Hall
FINANCIAL TIMES

In an increasingly competitive world, we believe it's quality of
thinking that gives you the edge – an idea that opens new
doors, a technique that solves a problem, or an insight that
simply makes sense of it all. The more you know, the smarter
and faster you can go.

That's why we work with the best minds in business and finance
to bring cutting-edge thinking and best learning practice to a
global market.

Under a range of leading imprints, including *Financial Times
Prentice Hall*, we create world-class print publications and
electronic products bringing our readers knowledge, skills and
understanding, which can be applied whether studying or at work.

To find out more about Pearson Education publications, or tell us
about the books you'd like to find, you can visit us at
www.pearsoned.co.uk

PEARSON

Inside the leader's mind

five ways to think like a leader

Liz Mellon

Financial Times
Prentice Hall
is an imprint of

Harlow, England • London • New York • Boston • San Francisco • Toronto
Sydney • Tokyo • Singapore • Hong Kong • Seoul • Taipei • New Delhi
Cape Town • Madrid • Mexico City • Amsterdam • Munich • Paris • Milan

PEARSON EDUCATION LIMITED

Edinburgh Gate
Harlow CM20 2JE
Tel: +44 (0)1279 623623
Fax: +44 (0)1279 431059
Website: www.pearsoned.co.uk

First published in Great Britain in 2011

© Pearson Education 2011

The right of Liz Mellon to be identified as author of this work has been asserted by her in accordance with the Copyright, Designs and Patents Act 1988.

Pearson Education is not responsible for the content of third party internet sites.

ISBN: 978-0-273-74418-4

British Library Cataloguing-in-Publication Data
A catalogue record for this book is available from the British Library

Library of Congress Cataloging-in-Publication Data
Mellon, Elizabeth.
  Inside the leader's mind : five ways to think like a leader / Liz Mellon.
     p. cm.
  Includes bibliographical references and index.
  ISBN 978-0-273-74418-4 (pbk.)
  1. Leadership. I. Title.
  HD57.7.M456 2011
  658.4'092--dc22

                                    2011003919

All rights reserved. No part of this publication may be reproduced, stored in a retrieval system, or transmitted in any form or by any means, electronic, mechanical, photocopying, recording or otherwise, without either the prior written permission of the publisher or a licence permitting restricted copying in the United Kingdom issued by the Copyright Licensing Agency Ltd, Saffron House, 6–10 Kirby Street, London EC1N 8TS. This book may not be lent, resold, hired out or otherwise disposed of by way of trade in any form of binding or cover other than that in which it is published, without the prior consent of the publisher.

ARP Impression 98

Typeset in Melior 9.5/13.5 by 30
Printed in Great Britain by Clays Ltd, St Ives plc

To Gary and Alexis

Contents

Acknowledgements

2010 WAS THE YEAR I SAID I'D GET HELP. So I found a trainer
to help me run the London Marathon (4 hours 30 minutes –
a respectable time – thank you, Sanjay). And a whole host of
people helped me to write this book – my second marathon
of 2010. It gives me enormous pleasure to thank them.

My first thank you has to be the 20 leaders who spent time
they didn't really have exploring my ideas with me and
sharing their stories for this book. They have more titles and
responsibilities than those listed here, but this is enough
detail for you to find them on the web.

- Tom Albanese, CEO of Rio Tinto;

- Clive Bannister, HSBC's Head of Insurance and a Group
  Managing Director (until April 2010);

- John Botts, Chairman of United Business Media;

- Irene Dorner, President and CEO of HSBC Bank USA;

- Niall FitzGerald KBE, Deputy Chairman of Thomson
  Reuters;

- Richard Fleck, Chairman of the Auditing Practices Board
  and senior advisor at Herbert Smith;

- Dominique Fournier, CEO, Infineum International Ltd;

- Kevin Kelly, CEO, Heidrick & Struggles;

- Rob Leith, CEO, Global Corporate and Investment
  Banking, Standard Bank;

- Ronnie Leten, CEO, Atlas Copco;

- Jacko Maree, Group CEO, Standard Bank;

- Rod Martin, Chairman and CEO of Alico;

- Dennis Nally, Chairman of the PwC International Network;

- Blair Sheppard, Dean of Duke University's Fuqua School of Business;

- Peter Shaw, Chief Risk Officer, RBS UK (2008);

- Martin Spurling, CEO, HSBC Bank Turkey;

- Paul Thurston, Chief Executive, HSBC Retail Banking and Wealth Management and a Group Managing Director of HSBC Group;

- Sim Tshabalala, Deputy CEO, Standard Bank Group;

- Sir John Tusa, Chairman of the University of the Arts, London;

- Jasmine Whitbread, international Chief Executive of Save the Children.

What I discovered in this process is not just how generous they are – but also how thoughtful. Each of them spent our time together to delve into their personal beliefs and deeply held values. Crystallising and continuing to develop their views about leadership is important to them and they found it worth spending time on. I admire their energy, openness and commitment to learning.

Colleagues inside and outside Duke Corporate Education sat with me and helped me to think through my ideas at various points along this journey. Randy White, a gifted leadership teacher, was unbelievably generous with his time and insights. He even read and commented on the manuscript (there is no greater love). My mentor and muse, Blair Sheppard, offered me great support and inspiration. Nedra Brasher spent her own time on research for me (to check that I wasn't reinventing somebody else's wheel). Jane Kasper helped me think through how to bring the ideas alive in the classroom. Jonathan Besser asked me nearly

every day 'How's the book coming? Oh, good!' Tim Last,
Rosemary Mathewson, Devin Bigoness and Ian Turner
introduced me to some of their favourite leaders.

I have the privilege to teach alongside some of the best
executive teachers on the planet, a constant source of
provocation and new ideas – Sudhanshu Palsule, Gary
Latham, Nandani Lynton and Maarten Asser. (Nandani,
Randy and I formed a Writers' Advisory Group – wag.)
Bob Rosen, John Viney, Gordon Hewitt, Maurice Saias,
Paul Willman and Dennis Baltzley let me pick their brains
in the early stages and compared notes with me about
their own experiences. Maurice Duffy, Mara Green, Mike
Canning, Cindy Emrich and Sara Nilsson DeHanas gave
me a platform to try out my ideas. Bob Reinheimer, a dear
colleague, kindly adopted my ideas to expand his already
formidable teaching range.

Randy recommended to me the CrainerDearlove
partnership. (They are as inseparable as Ant and Dec and it
is just as hard to remember which one is who.) Stuart and
Des are the midwives of ideas and I can confidently say
that without their help, I'd still be working on this book.
They sat with me three times and debated and questioned
until I was clear about what I was saying. Then I ran off to
write it between meetings. My editor at FT Prentice Hall,
Chris Cudmore, was similarly incredibly supportive and
endlessly helpful.

To live by my own creed, I should go back in time as
well as thanking current colleagues. One colleague who
commented on an early draft said 'there are echoes of Rob
and Gareth here'. This isn't surprising. I was lucky enough
to work at London Business School for 15 years and was
part of the talented group who worked in the department of
organisational behaviour. John Hunt led us in formulating
and testing our ideas about people at work. The company
of Nigel Nicholson, Rob Goffee, Gareth Jones, Jay Conger,

Tim Morris, Paul Willman and Lynda Gratton provided a hothouse for ideas.

In common with many part-time writers' friends and family, mine took a hit. On holiday, evenings and weekends people tiptoed around me as I sat, glued to the computer. They were forgiving when I failed to make events and supportive of my endurance. Pat McCann fed me on more than one occasion so that I wouldn't have to move. So to Gary, Alexis, Dan, John, Grace, Andreas, Mike, Avril, Crispin, Pauline, June and Jim – this is a promise that I'll be there next time. And to the wonderful Tim Jenkins, who paused between engagements with Elizabeth Hurley and Kylie Minogue to take my photograph for the book cover (I never realised you were so famous).

I have had such fun writing this book. Meeting new people, engaging in good quality debate and then sitting quietly, letting my thoughts evolve. I have discovered that I have endless patience for working and reworking ideas that I care about – I become engrossed for hours.

I shall miss the dogeared notebook that I have carried with me everywhere – literally, it has not left my side. And in the spirit of *on my watch*, let me close with a look to the future. I am already looking forward to the next book – with my daughter.

Foreword

LIZ MELLON CHALLENGES a central orthodoxy in the field
of leadership development. Construct a list of leadership
behaviours that are universally admired and consistently
measure individuals against that list. They will eventually
become highly effective leaders. In believing that we have
found the holy grail, we have overlooked one of the most
critical sources of a leader's competence – how they think.
After all, how I think determines how I will act. So let's put
the horses in front of the cart.

To help us understand how leaders think, Liz takes us into
the minds of senior-most leaders who are succeeding in
roles that are among the most demanding in today's fast
paced world. Using rich examples, she lays out each of
the states of mind that are trademarks of these remarkable
individuals. As a reader, it is a privilege to peer into the
minds of these masters of leadership and to learn from
them. You will get a textured picture of how they really
do think differently from many managers. For many of us,
these states of mind will be challenging even to entertain.
Yet they are products of the reality that enterprise leaders
face every day – worlds so complex, so dynamic that even
the most rigorously composed bar and pie charts cannot
provide clear answers.

Two of the mind states deeply reflect the demands of our
hyper-competitive global landscape – *no safety net* and
being *comfortable in discomfort*. The first is a high wire
act. As a senior leader, you have to have the courage to step
out first on the high wire – the wire of change, the wire
of future opportunity. It is a wire with no net to capture

you underneath. You could fail. The odds are good that at a minimum you will face significant setbacks. On the other hand, you realise that nothing will happen within your organisation unless you make that first move. Liz will powerfully remind you that you cannot delegate away change leadership to a group of middle management or front line leaders. It must start with you. As Liz importantly notes, this state of mind is not an impulsive one. It is a state where you have done your homework. You have listened to wise counsel. The second mind state – *comfortable in discomfort* – is a necessity in a world where you always have imperfect and incomplete information. Successful top leaders have learnt to love ambiguity rather than be frozen by it. You and I have to learn to move forward, to be decisive in a world where multiple solutions may work. These are not easy states of mind to cultivate. If you have been rewarded for rigorous analysis and meeting your 'plan' year after year with great precision, these mind states will seem foreign.

The third state of mind – *solid core* – captures the fact that leaders must have character, integrity, and a sense of humility. If you are going to lead well, you must be grounded in a set of core values that ensure your decisions and actions are consistent and that they set standards that others aspire to. Liz makes a wonderful comment about the fact that when managers in the business world are asked to identify leaders they turn to societal leaders like Mandela or Gandhi, not business leaders. Why? It is because they are exemplars of a society's greatest values. They live out in remarkable ways codes of conduct we hold dear. In an age where our images of business executives are shaped by cartoons such as Dilbert and TV shows like *The Boss*, you can begin to grasp why we hunger for the business leaders who possess genuine character and humility. Humility is one of a leader's greatest allies. It keeps you open to learning and keeps the sycophants at bay.

The fourth and fifth states of mind – *on my watch* and
I am the enterprise – are about institutional leadership. I
love Liz's notion that senior-most leaders have to think in
terms of their organisation's past, its present, and its future.
These are the three 'time zones' you lead across. Given
daily demands, it is all too easy to imagine yourself in the
middle zone – the present. I see all too many executives lost
in this zone. It is rare to find the executive who is thinking
out five years to a decade. It is rare to see the executive who
is courageous enough to make short-term sacrifices that in
the longer run ensure a healthy future for their organisation.
This mindset also depends on the fact that you recognise
your own mortality. As a result, you start developing the
next generation to replace yourself as soon as you step
into the role. The *I am the enterprise* state of mind is a bit
of a contradiction. While you need humility to lead, you
also need a robust ego. In Buddhism, there is a story that
captures the paradox. A young monk asks a very wise and
enlightened monk about the path to enlightenment. The
wise monk says simply that one needs ego to even believe
one can make the journey to enlightenment. Ego not only
gets you started on the road, it gives you the determination
to persist. But just before you can achieve actual
enlightenment, you must give up your ego. You need the
self-confidence and resilience that comes with the *I am the
enterprise* mind state to even assume you can lead a global
enterprise. But to stay adaptive in that journey, you will
also need humility to change course at critical junctures.
The *I am the enterprise* mindset also pushes us to accept
accountability for not only our own actions but those of the
organisation. The 'I' also powerfully reminds us that we set
the example, that our actions set the tone and the standards.
After all, these will be the measuring sticks that our
employees use to assess our leadership. At the same time,
can you accept the fact that the enterprise is more important
and more enduring than you are? This book highlights that

leading at the top is full of paradoxical states of mind. But exceptional leaders are able to keep these states in a healthy tension with one another.

My hope is that Liz Mellon's book will make you feel uncomfortable. That's exactly what she is hoping too. If you can get accustomed to that state by the time you finish reading this provocative and inspiring book, you will have achieved at least one of the mind states you need to succeed as a leader.

Jay A. Conger

Kravis Chaired Professor of Leadership Studies, Claremont McKenna College, California

Visiting Professor, London Business School

Author of Boardroom Realities *and* The Practice of Leadership

Introduction

never thought I would write another book on leadership. So why was I compelled to do so?

After all, a reservoir of ink has been spilt on the subject. Everyone has an opinion about what leadership is. We may not be able to agree on a description, but, like fine art, we all know a good leader when we see one. If you are in the spotlight as a leader, everything you do is dissected. And in today's globally wired world, we don't miss a thing.

And let's be clear – leadership is universal, whether you are the chief executive officer of a global company or the director of a local volunteer charity organisation. It makes a difference to lives and to organisations.

Leaders, would-be leaders and researchers have mulled this over for years. We've thought about the personality of a leader and we have concluded that personality alone can't explain why one person is a leader and another person is more likely to be a follower. We've spent a lot of time thinking about how a leader behaves, too. There is a profession that is dedicated to producing lists of leadership behaviours, so that we can literally measure effective leaders by watching them in action.

What is missing?

Yet, after 25 years devoted to leadership development, working throughout the world, I had a nagging feeling that something was missing. Somehow, I thought, we still haven't captured the essence of leadership.

I wasn't alone. Many leaders shared my views. In classroom session after classroom session, as I debated leadership with highly skilled, thoughtful and effective executives – all practising leaders – we constantly returned to a handful of important questions:

- Aren't some leaders naturally born to the task with innate qualities, which work and life experiences bring to the fore?

- If leaders can be developed, and we think we know which behaviours they should demonstrate, don't we risk producing clones?

- How does being developed to a menu of behaviours fit with authenticity? Isn't being true to yourself, the real you, a vital characteristic for every leader?

- Why do about 60 per cent of leaders derail?

- Where do morals, ethics and good character fit into all of this?

For all the books and all the analysis, the questions surrounding leadership are substantial and important. As I have tried out these questions and discussed them with leaders all over the world, I have, slowly but surely, seen a new idea emerge.

We have overlooked how leaders think. Yet it is how we think that determines if and how we act. And I have found that effective leaders, irrespective of race, age or gender, think in remarkably similar ways.

Inside the Leader's Mind is your guide to my global journey, my restless questioning of leaders and the resulting ideas which, I hope, will accelerate your own leadership journey.

Liz Mellon, London, November 2010

chapter

1

Five ways of thinking like a leader

et's cut to the chase. The reason we can't capture the essence of leadership is because we have focused too hard on behaviour – naturally enough, because it's easy to see and measure.

What we have overlooked is how leaders think.

This became clearer and clearer in the hundreds of hours of conversation I had to form this book. As the conversations progressed and I started to make sense of them, I began to hear a different pattern of ideas from those who were at the top, or destined for the top.

Successful careers are built on a mixture of experience and skills, but that combination is not enough. And it is incredibly hard to capture the full range of behaviours that in different combinations equate to leadership – the variety of human nature is just too broad. Behaviour alone cannot forecast good leadership.

> the most successful leaders think in remarkably similar ways

What I found is that the most successful leaders think in remarkably similar ways: in five remarkably similar ways, in fact.

Testing new ideas

I took these five ways of thinking out to a select group of leaders and asked for their reactions. They were overwhelmingly positive. As one remarked: 'What you have done is to describe what happens in practice and then to derive principles from it. It's a very interesting approach – and that is not a throwaway line. You are on to something here.'

I tested out the five ways of thinking with CEOs and chairmen/women of companies, charities and universities. I was looking for diversity of opinion. And as much as possible, I tell the story through theirs. I hope to bring the ideas alive with their anecdotes and experiences. The quotations, whether attributed or not, are all theirs.

You won't find descriptions and definitions of these ways of thinking in other books about leadership or personal development. Experts and executives have been so focused on monitoring how leaders behave that we have all but overlooked how leaders think.

> these ways of thinking can help you to be
> a better leader

My firm and passionate belief is that these ways of thinking can help you to be a better leader.

Informal assessment

The five ways of thinking provide a shorthand for you to understand better your own leadership and how and what you need to develop – a self-assessment framework, if you like. They will also help you to think about leaders that you guide and mentor.

When I share the five ways of thinking with leaders, I ask them to apply them to themselves. But next, they often start musing about their own executive team, using the five ways as a simple assessment tool. They identify someone who has three of the ways of thinking already, with potential to develop further. They then pinpoint another person who is a good solid team member, but they are conscious that they might never be able to develop this kind of thinking. It isn't that this is their first assessment of the individual. But it gives them the language to articulate easily their insight about different people on their team.

You will notice that the executives I interviewed are very senior. They run multi-million-dollar/euro (choose your currency) global enterprises. People in these very senior executive positions have evolved their thinking to a different level. This doesn't mean that less elevated senior executives (say, those in the top 30, rather than in the top 5) think in unacceptable, or inadequate, ways. Not at all. They, too, are strong and effective players, who have assimilated and learnt from experience over the years. They have that job close to the top because they have earned it.

Underlying each of these chief executive ways of thinking is perfectly acceptable senior executive thinking.

Move beyond thinking like a senior executive

The problem is, thinking like a senior executive will get you close to the top, but no further. You'll remain one of those assessed as a solid team member, but lacking the capacity to move further upwards.

People in the search business – the firms who specialise in finding chief executives and board members for their clients – will tell you that there is a big difference between the top 50 and the handful of the most senior leaders in a global organisation. Some of these enterprises are huge. They can employ anything from 50,000 to 350,000 people, working across

80 or more countries. So differentiating between the top 50 and the top 10 sounds like a bit of an exaggeration, when all the senior leaders in these giant enterprises must exercise large amounts of responsibility. But when you get up close, you can see the difference. This 'good, but insufficient for the top job' thinking gets you just so far. As we'll explore in Chapter 7, 'Keep on developing', it's as much about wanting to be a leader – and accepting all the hard work and endurance that goes with the job – as it is about talent.

> evolving your thinking will take you
> to the next step

The next step is about moving you still further forward in your leadership journey. Each of the five ways of thinking provides a step forward to a more senior role. Evolving your thinking will take you to the next step. This doesn't mean that you abandon everything you know – far from it. It means that you stretch to the next level. It's time to stop relying on generic leadership advice, which is often pretty formulaic and quite basic for many high performing executives. If you make it into the top 50, you know you are doing well. The next step is nuanced, to say the least.

Dance steps

And these five ways of thinking, taken together, can help you step safely across the threshold to inspiring leadership.

You don't need to take these steps in any particular order, although they are set out as a numbered sequence below. Think of them as dance steps to be mastered. They aren't steps to be laboriously climbed or arduously sequenced. Leaders try to think in all five ways simultaneously.

Five steps to move upwards

Step one – no safety net

As a senior executive, you already have a well-developed and business-minded outlook. You understand the need to balance risk and reward, you are pragmatic and you make sure that you both consult and advise.

The next step is to recognise that you are alone.

It's not that you lose the ability to take advice. But you know that if you don't push the boundaries, no-one else will and you will slowly but surely sow the seeds of failure. You are at the edge of uncertainty. Others can advise you, but they can't reassure you, because you are trying something that hasn't been tried before. You are willing to lean into unknown risk and take the step that so many others fear. And you are not waiting for permission or for someone else to ask you to take it on. You are going to do it anyway. It's a high wire act, balancing fear and adrenalin. Except that, unlike the circus performer, you have no safety net, no-one to catch you if you fall. And even knowing this, you still step out into the unknown. You embrace the risk.

'No-one explains that doing what you are told is not enough. You have to be more than a good soldier.' (CEO) **Your next step is to move the organisation into uncharted territory.**

Step two – comfortable in discomfort

As an executive, you can take a decision and stand by it. You have learnt to gather and quickly synthesise data and make the call – you are smart and decisive. Over the years, you have honed these decision-making skills and you know that being decisive is an important part of your job. Where some dither, you move to action. You have become quicker and more fluid in the decisions you take.

At the very senior level, the complexity of the situations and decisions you face expands rapidly. There is rarely 'one best way'; there are options, with different probabilities attached. It is a more multi-layered and confusing world. Instead of the decision being between A and B, sometimes it has to be 'A plus B'. There is still data – reams – but the data can't make the call, the decision can be argued either way. It is much less clear.

Now comes the moment where you understand that stopping to gather yet more data won't cut it. Sometimes the decision has to be taken without full information, or you risk being left behind and putting the enterprise at risk. Sometimes the opposite is true; others are pushing for a decision based on the data, but your instinct tells you to hold off deciding until the time feels right. You must live with the discomfort of knowing that the solution is not easy or straightforward. It's increasingly a grey world where you have to think 'yes, and', not 'either, or'. To develop this way of thinking, you must learn to live with ambiguity, even to thrive on it. You can consume the tension and the uncertainty doesn't disable you.

'You can analyse nine ways to Sunday, but you don't have time and the world is too complicated.' (CEO) **Your next step is to move beyond the data and make a judgement call.**

Step three – solid core

Everyone wants a confident leader and, as a seasoned executive, you look the part. You exude confidence. When you say 'let's go', people follow because they believe that you can lead them somewhere better. Your leadership seems joined up and consistent; you have presence and stature. You seem authentic.

To take the next step is to think in a way that adds an inner sense of purpose and strength to your authenticity. It is a heightened sense of integrity and it is strongly driven from within. This means that, whether you have a clear strategic direction for the future or not, you have a strong sense of knowing, from within, the right thing to do. That is, you may or may not know exactly where you are leading others, because today's complex world is sometimes too ambiguous for clarity, but you know where you are coming from. This gives you the strength, self insight and capability to move. Whether it is instinct, experience or something else, you understand the right thing to do. You are grounded and calm, and have a clear sense of purpose and direction from within.

'A bunch of it is about the soul. Take me as I am, I will say what needs to be said.' (CEO) **Your next step is to trust your inner compass to guide you to do the right thing.**

Step four – on my watch

You spend the majority of your time, as a successful senior executive, making sure that the business stays on track and afloat. You listen to advice that suggests you try to be more strategic and look ahead, but in reality 70 per cent of your time is spent fixing the here and now. This is vital work and it keeps the organisation in business. The analysts are going to be unforgiving if you miss the beat on the next quarter's results and you take this responsibility seriously.

The next step isn't just to spend more time thinking about the future. It is more complex than that. Of course, you do have to shift to spending more time focusing on building the future, which means leaving a lot more of the 'here and now' to others. But there is an important nuance here. You also need to integrate the past into a broadened perspective on time.

It's not just about where the organisation is heading, but also about making sure that you integrate the past into your future. You need to capture specific elements of the enterprise heritage, so that you can help others to understand the bigger purpose, the broader story, and see what is unique about your organisation. It's not simply about respecting and honouring the past. You must show respect for what got the enterprise to this point in its life, but you must also be able to let the past go if it might harm the future. You respect the past and integrate its story into the present, but you can also move away from it, change the direction. You want to sustain success beyond your time in the organisation.

'I am an historian. I spend about 50 per cent of my time on the present, but only as a way of knitting it all together and linking it to the future.' (CEO) **Your next step is to become a steward, so that success continues after your watch.**

Step five – I am the enterprise

In your senior role, you already know that you are good at getting things done; you deliver results. This is a key reason for your success. You are happy to step forward and to be held accountable. You understand how the business works and that's another reason why you are good at your job. You deliver the results that are asked of you in your area of the organisation and sometimes you even beat your targets.

Now it's time to extend your thinking. No longer just think about your part of the business, start to think about the impact of your actions and decisions on the whole business. This means across the enterprise, outside of your domain of control. You should come to represent the whole enterprise.

When you take a decision, you are willing to miss, reduce or exceed your personal targets if you can see that it would be better for the whole organisation. You understand deeply, not just what the business does, but what it stands for, what it means to be part of this enterprise. And you represent it faithfully, out to the world and back inside the organisation. You live its values as if they were your own; everything you say and do embodies what the enterprise stands for. You manage yourself carefully so that you are always delivering what followers need. It's more than being a role model – you commit wholeheartedly. Everything you do, and everything you don't do, creates, sustains or modifies the enterprise.

'Everything you do must be for the organisation.' (CEO) **Your next step is to represent the enterprise faithfully, as if you were one and the same**.

Where does this thinking come from?

These five ways of thinking shape and structure the rest of this book. But before we delve further into their meaning and just how they affect leaders, and your leadership, let's pause to consider the context facing you today.

Change in the world has accelerated to warp speed. Globalisation started 20 years ago. Before that, we had international firms, or multinational firms, but they really lacked the scale and agility of today's global enterprises. Today, many are operating in 80-plus countries and employ hundreds of thousands of people. This scale has brought with it complexity of every kind – cultural, economic, social, political and technological. Some of these leaders carry iPads to surf the web or read books. Technology has linked us globally, but also put us under pressure to cope with new information 24/7. We are connected and communicating constantly. If you don't keep up, you get left behind very fast. Investors can be fickle, even if customers aren't. So speed and complexity govern leaders' lives.

This brings the obvious question – have successful leaders evolved these five ways of thinking because of these new pressures? And the answer is, I don't know.

Some of the leaders told me that they have always thought in this way, since they were aged 15 or so (and are now 50-plus).

Others said that they have developed one or more of these ways of thinking slowly over the years – they come with experience and maturity. We don't know the answer. But what we do know is that, if you don't think in these five ways, you risk getting left behind.

> if you don't yet think in the same way, you have the potential to do so

So I can't tell you when and how these leaders developed these ways of thinking – and nor can they. The way they did it is as individual as they are. The important message that I want you to hear is that, if you don't yet think in the same way, you have the potential to do so.

An example of the five in action

As much as possible, the story will be told through the words of the leaders who think in these five ways. It's generally better straight from the source, isn't it?

Let's start with PricewaterhouseCoopers (PwC). This is a global audit and consulting firm, which was formed in 1998 from a merger between Price Waterhouse and Coopers & Lybrand. PwC has a history in client services that dates back to the nineteenth century. Each accounting practice originated in London during the mid 1800s and now they employ more than 163,000 people in 151 countries.

Dennis Nally has been Chairman and Senior Partner of PwC LLP, the United States firm, since 2002. In March 2009, Dennis was elected Chairman of the PwC International Network – effectively the global firm – for a four-year term. It's challenging to reach the top in any organisation. It's extremely tough in a partnership like PwC, because it's your peers who vote on you. Each partner is a capable and strong-minded individual, and gaining their respect across the board is a feat.

Now, of course, it's true in any organisation that once you are within spitting distance of the top, the leader who emerges is the one who commands the respect of peers. (If you think you get chosen by the Board or the chairman, think again. Your peers will either follow you or they won't. Even if the Board appoints you, your peers will vote with their feet and you won't last long if they don't rate you.) It's just that the situation is even more pointed when your partners, essentially your co-owners, choose you. Thousands of them have to vote for you. It's a tremendous accolade.

Dennis is a calm character. He is measured and thoughtful in his responses. I swear he keeps a picture in his attic (like Dorian Grey) because every time I see him he looks younger. Because he is calm and always looks happy, sometimes he can be a bit hard to read. His voice has an almost boyish energy and light when he talks about his work. He just loves it.

The way I think

Dennis said this about these five ways of thinking: 'This is exactly the way I think about this from a leadership standpoint today. Not like before. I used to never ask a question where I didn't know the answer. I used to spend all my time on business today, where I am accountable, and not 5–10 years out, when someone else will be successful. I have never seen this put on a piece of paper so concisely. Here is the leadership challenge.' Dennis is an advocate of the five ways.

He recently led an extensive review of PwC's global structure, which resulted in significant enhancements to the global Network, which were implemented in late 2008. In 2009 it was announced that in his new role as Chairman, he would continue to serve on the PwC Network Leadership Team along with his successor as Chairman of PwC US; Ian Powell, Chairman of PwC UK; Silas Yang, Chairman of PwC China Hong Kong; and Hans Wagener, Chairman of PwC Germany.

The project he led to review the global structure was called the Network of the Future and the internal task force worked on it for two-and-a-half years. 'A small group of about 15 people looked at how the firm was going forwards. We met for eight to nine months and debated and suggested. There was no right answer, no wrong answer, no roadmap. Intuitively, the solution we arrived at made sense and I knew this is where we needed to go, but I had to sell it with facts – not intuition. If this had not been approved, I would have been done. But even for tough projects like this, I love what I do and I have energy around it.'

These smart chief executives always pack a lot of ideas into a few sentences, so let's de-code this. It appears that Dennis had a lot at stake personally here, and that, if this strategic project had not been successful, it could have been a career-limiting move for him. His partners and colleagues, who have a choice, would not have followed him. That sounds like *no safety net*.

Then, it makes intuitive sense to him, even though he has to justify it with analysis and facts. So it feels like the right thing to do and an inner instinct tells him that it's a good move. Doing the right thing is a clear example of a *solid core*. 'There was no right answer, no wrong answer, no roadmap.' So this isn't a straight choice between A and B. It sounds more as if the data isn't going to guide the decision and that Dennis was operating in ambiguous circumstances. He would not have been able to do so had he not been *comfortable in discomfort*. He and his colleagues are working today to build a long-term sustainable future for the organisation tomorrow. He's thinking *on my watch*. And finally, the personal risk he's taking doesn't worry him and he is ready to invest his energy into acting for the good of the whole. He is thinking *I am the enterprise*.

This is a lot of information packed into a short couple of paragraphs. As you read the chapters, laying out these five ways of thinking in more detail, it will make more sense.

It's a menu, not a recipe

Unlike so much advice that drives towards the 'one best way' to build the effective leader, this is a menu from which you can find your personal differentiator.

The stories of these CEOs and chairmen/women, which will be set out in the coming chapters, are varied. If these leaders ever found themselves in the unlikely position of being in exactly the same situation, the decisions they might take could be diametrically opposed. They certainly wouldn't react in the same way as each other, or behave alike. But they would think in the same way.

This is not a behavioural recipe, or a cookie cutter for success. It is a menu – and what you choose and how you react will be as individual as you are. It allows you to be truly authentic. This is liberating. Thinking like a leader is a bit like the slogan 'Intel Inside'. Just like the hardware we never see inside the 'black box' of a computer, thinking like this from the inside can power greater leadership effectiveness.

Where are you in your leadership journey?

How do you take the next step in your own leadership journey? I imagine that you have worked hard and learnt the fundamentals. Along the way you have gathered a rich mix of experiences and can truthfully say much of the time 'I have seen this before'. You have accepted, learnt from, and then excelled at more and more difficult challenges. You know your business and have clear ideas about what it takes to lead it. You have a legitimate, hard-won view of the universe within which you operate. You know how it goes.

Yet the moment this thinking shapes your ideas, the moment you feel you've 'made it', is exactly the moment to pause and reconsider. When you think you know, this is just the time to challenge yourself. The success formulas that have served you well will constrain you. In fact, the more successful you have been, the more unlikely you are to see past the way you lead now. As the Chinese proverb goes, habits are cobwebs at first, cables at last.

> when you think you know, this is just the time to challenge yourself

Don't let your experience to date hold you back, but use it as a springboard to the next stage in your leadership journey. Your ability to change will depend on your capacity to move away from your comfort zone. You'll see from the stories in this book that even CEOs keep on developing, learning and growing.

Before you dive into the rest of the book, why don't you ask yourself a couple of questions first, questions that executives most often ask themselves about their next stage of development?

▌ Where do you need to concentrate most on the five ways of thinking to help you to prepare for your next, bigger, leadership challenge?

▌ Which way of thinking do you think would add most value to your current repertoire?

▌ Which way of thinking will be the easiest for you to develop (start here if you can)?

This simple exercise will give you a way to move around the book and focus on the sections that are most important for you.

Just when you think you've arrived – a new leadership journey is beginning. Your next step is to adopt five new ways of thinking.

A final thought

So, put simply, you need to think differently about your job. We don't always frame our experience using exactly the same words. But, when we hear an approach that works – that describes our experience in ways that make it come alive, that make it understandable, that make it accessible – then we can reflect, understand and communicate. This framework describing five different ways of thinking helps leaders to discuss the experience of leading in complex global organisations in a way that is real and that makes sense to them.

It is a deeply intense and personal way of understanding why leading others is such a difficult thing to do. This book can help you to be better at doing so.

chapter 2

No safety net

n the last chapter, we looked at the five ways in which leaders think. Now we will start to look at each one in turn, in more depth. Why are we starting with *no safety net*? Because this is where it starts – with your inner conviction that you will take the step that others may fear, or that they may not even see. You set out understanding that you are the one who will take the responsibility and step into the unknown to make it happen.

The bus is leaving

We are on a bus and it is getting dark. The road is bad, with lots of potholes, so we sway and lurch along uncomfortably. We have been planting mangroves and the mosquitoes have had a field day with us, so we are feeling virtuous but sore. Now we are on our way back to the hotel.

There are 30 of us on a strategy training programme in Kuala Lumpur in Malaysia. I am sitting on the bus next to Clive Bannister, the executive sponsoring the training programme, and talking with him about leadership – his leadership. Clive is a compelling character. Formerly head of the private banking business at HSBC, he took charge of their insurance business from 2006 to 2010. Before joining them, he had been a partner in the financial consulting practice of Booz Allen & Hamilton and a personal advisor to their former CEO and Chairman,

Sir John Bond. He also happens to be the son of Roger Bannister, famous for running the world's first sub-four-minute mile. Clive has certainly inherited the stamina and drive of his father and has a well-deserved reputation for taking charge and making things happen.

Being in the top ten is very different

In our conversation, Clive is not only smart but also intellectual, well-read and knowledgeable. Yet he never once shows impatience for those who can't think at his speed, quite the opposite. Followers love him. He goes out of his way to thank people for their contribution and is unfailingly courteous to everyone from the doorman and beyond. It was his idea to plant the mangroves, to get these high-paid executives out into the real world of sweat and effort. He was working in the rarefied atmosphere of the very top of the global bank. There is a real difference between being in the top 50 and the top 10,[1] the difference between thinking like a successful senior executive and thinking like a CEO. Clive was in the top 10. I am fascinated to hear his ideas.

I struggle to see in the dark, to take notes, not start to feel bus sick and look interested, all at the same time. I am not sure that I am even going to be able to read my notes back. He is passionate about his subject and doesn't seem to mind or notice.

'I grew the business for the bank,' he said. 'The CEO knows that I get stuff done. This means taking chances, but I reduce risk because I know the business inside out, I understand where others in the industry are placed and I can quickly see where to take some chances. Now I have taken on the job of growing this new business line for the bank. Nothing ventured, nothing gained.'

Measured risk-taking

So there is immediate confirmation of Clive's reputation for
building business and making change happen. That's why
he kept being put in to lead critical parts of the business.
And he is clearly up for some measured risk-taking, stepping
forward to take responsibility and taking some chances that
the competition aren't or daren't. He went on: 'There are some
orthodoxies in this business that cry out to be challenged,
so I am making one or two moves that directly address our
customers' concerns and are seen to add value to them. Do I
always have my CEO's approval? No – but then do I need it?'

Clive relishes momentum and the adventure of change. We know
that leaders make change happen – that's why we need them.[2]
But there is more to this story. He is ready to take chances,
without concern for his personal situation. He is ready to act
without instruction and without approval, even from his CEO.
He uses experience and knowledge as a guide, but is willing to
move beyond the known into unknown territory, challenging
orthodoxies, that is, challenging the usually accepted ways of
doing business, in order to gain competitive advantage.

It's a high wire act

The best metaphor here is the circus act. Whether it's a high
wire walk or a trapeze, you are working at height and you have
chosen to do it without a safety net.

Let's start from the position of a senior executive, where the
package already looks good. You can take advice as well as
give it and you are more than happy to accept accountability.
You run a big chunk of the business and you probably have
a reputation as a safe pair of hands. You feel a strong sense
of ownership and present ideas and actions as enterprise
decisions, not your own. So far, so good. But let's think about

how what you have learnt as a senior executive might hold you back. Any transition means learning something new. It also often means giving up something that you have already learnt, because it just won't work at the next level.

Here is what is missing.

it's your job to push the boundaries

It's your job to push the boundaries, to make the case for driving forward into the unknown. Don't wait to be asked or told. See the opportunity and lead to seize it. Think *no safety net*.

There are five pieces to *no safety net*. The first is to recognise you are alone, because no-one else is likely to see the opportunities that you can, or have the courage to grasp them. The second is to be brave enough to take that first step into the unknown, while (third) ensuring that you don't get too far ahead of everyone else. The fourth step is to keep alert to danger through maintaining a healthy sense of self doubt, but lastly, you can't be afraid to fail. You are leading. One CEO said: 'I want my people to know that the limit comes from inside, the ceiling is inside your own mind – you are the one holding yourself back.'

Adrenalin, but no fear – and *no safety net*.

You are alone

In the interviews, of the five ways of thinking, *no safety net* was often the one that grabbed the leaders' attention first. Most often the reaction was instinctive and positive. These senior leaders love the adventure of breaking new ground and moving the organisation forward. They know that it is up to them. If they don't push forward, no-one else is about to.

Every single one had a story about a new idea, a new business, a new structure – essentially, a 'first'. The refrain was all about it being the first time something had been tried. It would have filled two books; it's a shame there is only room for a couple of examples here.

As a senior leader, you have never been busier, worked so hard or commanded so many resources. You will have an executive team, thousands reporting to you, the attention of analysts and shareholders and probably a retinue of advisors – for example, a communications expert, a lawyer, a merger and acquisitions specialist and an industry strategist. You will never have been so surrounded by good advice. You will keep your mind as open as possible and listen as hard as you can.

And, in the middle of all that noise and bustle, you will never have been so alone.

No-one rings the CEO

As one leader put it, 'You look to the left and you look to the right and you realise that everyone is looking back at you.' You know that you see opportunities that others may not. And you are willing to take risks that others may not. You can take all the advice you want, but in the end, at this level, it's your call. When the Board asks for a decision, you take it. When the shareholders complain, it's you who decides what to do about it. The final call, along with the accountability, rests with you.

Ronnie Leten, the CEO of Atlas Copco, has an interesting story in Chapter 6, 'I am the enterprise', and we'll meet him fully there. Atlas Copco is an engineering company that manufactures and distributes compressors, generators, construction and mining equipment and industrial tools all over the world (in 174 countries). Ronnie was eloquent on this idea of being alone. 'When I ran the compressor business for Atlas Copco, I was the seventh biggest customer of Belgium telecom. I was always on the phone to people.' He gestured towards his phone, which had sat silently on the table between us for the entire interview. 'No-one calls the CEO – the phone just doesn't ring. If the business isn't going well, you question yourself – is it me, or us? As you build up more confidence in the role, you can take more "alone-ness".'

> as you build up more confidence in the role, you can take more "alone-ness"

This anecdote shows graphically how big the switch can be – from being constantly in touch when he was running the business that generates 50 per cent of the revenue for Atlas Copco, to the relative isolation of becoming CEO of the whole company.

It's even worse in a crisis

Rod Martin is the Chairman and CEO of Alico (American Life Insurance Company). After its parent AIG was bailed out by the US government to the tune of $182.5 billion in 2008,[3] AIG determined to sell Alico to help pay off the debt. Originally, it had been planned to float Alico on the stock exchange in an initial public offering (IPO), but by March 2010 the plan was to sell it to MetLife, Inc, one of the world's largest and most diversified international life insurance companies. We all read about the bankruptcies that shocked the world following the financial services' crisis – but probably less about the very human aftermath and fight for regeneration and survival.

Rod led Alico through this, the biggest crisis in its 90-year history, as plans for its future changed rapidly. He put in place four core beliefs to guide the organisation through the crisis: the future is in our hands (we are not passive victims); we are the 'we' (the answer is in the room with us); Alico is worth fighting for; this is our time. The challenges facing Alico were unprecedented and there were no case studies or career experiences to rely on. This was uncharted territory. And there were moments when everyone was fatigued.

What kept Rob going? Nineteen million customers and 12,000 employees to safeguard. As one of his team said, 'There were times when Rod had to talk us back in off the ledge'.

What are Rod's reflections on all of this? 'I probably never felt more alone than I did at times in this crisis. There were moments and days when I knew that this core group of people were looking at me and to me. It was the biggest test I have ever faced.'

Everything is exacerbated by crisis – but probably nothing more than this sense of being alone.

In conversation, these leaders would often talk about 'we' until it came to the big decision itself. That's when 'I' re-asserted itself. You are flying solo, ahead of the pack, as you move the organisation forwards, or the market propels you, into the unknown.

Take the first step

Taking the first step across the abyss, from here to the future, is hard. It takes courage. But let's face it, change is part of the job. As a leader, unless you are making change happen, it won't happen around you. We know that leaders distinguish themselves through having the courage to take the tough decisions, make the difficult stands.

The first step is to accept the role of challenger. Paul Thurston is a Group Managing Director of HSBC Group, and Chief Executive, HSBC Retail Banking and Wealth Management (we'll hear his story in the next chapter). As Paul says, 'Thirty-five years in HSBC and I guess you'd say I have a lot invested here. But I've always thought I could make a living at something else if it didn't work out for me. I have never been afraid to challenge conventional wisdom or to make changes that are needed, however unpopular they may be. What's the worst that could happen?'

Sim Tshabalala, Deputy CEO of the Standard Bank Group, agrees and his story is a great example of accepting challenge. This South African headquartered bank was established in 1862 and was linked to Standard Chartered Bank until 1987, during the apartheid years, when complete ownership of the Standard Bank Group was transferred to South Africa. They started expanding further into Africa at this time and in 2005 expanded their horizons internationally by buying BankBoston Argentina. In 2007, they became one of the forerunners of the so-called South–South connection, where trade flows take place between countries south of the equator, when the Industrial and Commercial Bank of China (ICBC) took a 20 per cent shareholding. As the centre of global business continues to move from West (USA) to East (China), it also moves from North to South. Business and governments are increasingly aware of the new pattern of South–South business activity and investments.

Sim is one of the new wave CEOs, younger, sometimes much younger, than the generation ahead of them. He ranks as one of the youngest amongst peers like Andrew Witty of GSK, Tony Hayward (former CEO of BP) and Tom Albanese of Rio Tinto. As we sit chatting in the Standard Bank's Global Leadership Centre in Johannesburg, Sim's almost boyish face is in strong contrast to his statesmanlike demeanour and deeply thoughtful responses. In the cool, grey room with the blinds drawn against the hot South African sun, he has almost a preternatural air of calm about him. He is warm and approachable – early success has not spoiled him. He lives his work and home life guided by some of the strongest values. A lawyer by training, Sim joined the bank in 2000. Let's hear his story.

The first story – Transformation in South Africa

Living in Africa and working globally, Sim sees part of his broader role as helping Africa – the so-called 'forgotten continent' to establish itself in the world. He wants to contribute to building the Rainbow Nation. After their first fully democratic election in 1994, the Rainbow Nation was how Bishop Desmond Tutu described the post-apartheid era in South Africa. The phrase means to capture the idea of multiculturalism in a country that had previously been identified with only two colours, black and white, strictly divided. President Nelson Mandela subsequently described South Africa as 'a rainbow nation, at peace with itself and the world'.[4]

As a black man, Sim is deeply committed to Transformation. This is a huge political and economic agenda for South Africa. It encompasses many facets of daily life, including embedding democracy and improving the situation for economically and socially disadvantaged black South Africans, so that they can achieve equal prosperity.

Take the risk

Sim says: 'I do move the enterprise into uncharted territory. I argue, for example, for finding ways to bank the unbanked. Without being immodest or uncharitable, we are way ahead of the other South African banks in this. It could be a spectacular failure – if it's right, it will work, if not, it will be a disaster.' We are straight into it. Here is the familiar story of arguing for something new – a first – and for taking a big risk, with a big potential upside, but also a big potential downside.

Sim wants to stretch the provision of financial services to previously under-serviced lower-income customers (profitably) in South Africa and all of Africa. His intent is to provide a long-term boost to the economic growth of the country, and the continent, as previously under-banked customers get the benefits of having access to credit. Their money is not so safe where they have classically banked it – under the mattress.

Banking the previously unbanked is a way of pulling forward the socially disadvantaged. It's right at the heart of the Transformation agenda. So, for Sim, this is more than just business. It's about building the future of the nation.

'Right now, I am heavily involved in the negotiations on the new phase of the Financial Sector Charter. They have been collapsing and reviving and I am dragging people to agree on some scary things, in order to avoid prescribed lending.' Sim is describing a 20-year tug of war between banks and the South African government. The government has been frustrated with the low level of bank lending and tried to introduce legislation to compel banks to lend, to get the poor into the housing market. Rather than be subjected to levels of lending prescribed by the government, which could have serious implications for bank profitability, the banks decided to create a Financial Sector Charter. Its aim is to transform the financial sector, increase investment and extend lending into the low-income housing market. If the negotiations fail, the government can be expected to step in and pass legislation to compel action.

Sim continued: 'For example, the principle that black people should own 25 per cent of institutions. There is a technical argument over the percentages that should be held directly and indirectly. I am arguing against a 15 per cent direct holding, because of the potentially crippling costs to the organisations. Instead, let's take the money and split it among the activities that are natural to financial services firms. Let's lend to small and medium size enterprises and co-operatives; let's finance new infrastructure in townships and rural areas.'

Again, let's get the complicated explanation out of the way so that we can understand what this means for Sim. He is arguing that instead of funding share ownership, some available finance should be redirected towards investment in small and medium sized enterprises and the like. These small ventures can stimulate employment and earnings, in a way that lending to foster the more passive activity of share ownership cannot.

Don't take it personally

What's the bottom line here? Why is this business proposition causing Sim such concern? 'I have been called Anti-Transformation for this. That's hard for a black man to face.' Sometimes taking the first step is even harder, because it's more than just business. It goes to the roots of our identity, how we see ourselves as a human being.

But Sim is also a businessman. He doesn't want legislation to curtail appropriate business venturing. He knows that the government wants the banking sector to extend lending and he is in agreement. But he has well-founded business views of the best way to do this, unbounded by political rhetoric. He wants to build an inclusive nation and fight against ongoing disparity of wealth and the trend towards a growing gap between the rich and the poor in some countries. And that means arguing against some of the more populist ideas that may not prove economically viable in the future – ideas that may even make the situation worse, not better. And he is willing to stand up and say so.

> you need to stay calm and keep your eye on the main purpose

Luckily for most of us, taking the first step into the unknown is a business adventure, not a cause for soul-searching about our identity. Few of us would find ourselves in Sim's shoes. What we can learn from Sim is that even when the going gets really tough, even when your detractors (and there will always be some) use the most emotional language – you need to stay calm and keep your eye on the main purpose. Sim knows that he has to help Standard Bank move forwards into new and untested business ventures. He cannot allow himself to be deterred by accusations that hurt him personally.

A second story – going global

Jasmine Whitbread was appointed as the first international Chief Executive of Save the Children in March 2010. This was a promotion from the previous role she held as Chief Executive of Save the Children UK, from 2005 when she joined the organisation. Before joining Save the Children, Jasmine spent six years with Oxfam, first as Regional Director in West Africa, and then as International Director responsible for Oxfam's programmes worldwide. Prior to this, she was Managing Director of a Thomson Financial business, based in the US. Her background is in international marketing in the technology sector.

Jasmine is a no-nonsense kind of woman. She is thoughtful but pretty intuitive, so she doesn't spend a lot of time on introspection. And she doesn't care much for overelaborate models of leadership. So it's well worth hearing what she has to say.

'We have agreed to create one Save the Children globally out of the 29 existing entities. We will take all our programmes from 50 countries and hand them over to the new entity containing the 29. We are deep into uncertainty, this is uncharted territory. At the end of the day it is clearly the right thing to do, so you just have to do it. The choice is to do it in the best way possible.'

Clarity and conviction

There is such clarity and certainty in her conviction. (She does describe herself as 'off the scale' decisive.) She is busy creating a global organisation. The uncertainty and complexity involved in this is enormous in any business. Being in the charity world adds another level of complexity. Charities survive because they rely to a great extent on volunteers, who all have their individual views of how the charity should be run and the special interests that it should serve. So gaining alignment is even harder than in business. It's a bit like trying to build just one political party from a roomful of conviction politicians.

There were tens of stories just like this. Senior leaders biting off big chunks of challenge, with enjoyment. All ready to take the first step.

Don't get too far ahead

So taking the first step doesn't seem to be too difficult for these leaders, even though the risks are big. However, as you step out across the abyss towards the bright new future that you can see so clearly, remember that not everyone is as clear-sighted as you.

Let's meet Kevin Kelly, CEO of Heidrick & Struggles, the global leadership advisory firm. During his career as a search consultant, Kevin has helped form corporate leadership teams for some of the world's most innovative companies. He is a well-known radical in his industry. He got his MBA from Duke and went on to join their Board of Visitors. He has written books about what the top job entails, including his own.[5] Kevin gives generously of his time to Duke. When we sat together at one of the Board of Visitors meetings in Durham, North Carolina, he was not only willing to give an interview, which he made time for immediately. He has gone out of his way to support this research. Kevin is one of those people who, when you email him, responds straight away. I always find that impressive in people who have big, busy jobs. Says a lot about how much energy they have.

Dramatic change

Kevin explains the changes he is making. 'In the last 12 months we have started contributing to organisations, not just offering placement. Leadership advisory is different, an evolution of the search industry. Eighteen months ago it was bumpy and we were bringing people along.'

The period he was talking about was January 2009, a time of deep recession. In times like that, few companies risk making big changes – they are generally consolidating and regrouping for the next upturn. Kevin is one of the foresighted CEOs who saw the downturn as an opportunity to restructure his business and position it for growth.

Heidrick & Struggles is in the process of transforming its business to become a Leadership Advisory firm. This means not only focusing on the acquisition of talent, which is historically the search business, but also on retention, development, assessment, and succession planning. This dramatic change will be achieved through both organic and inorganic growth.

So what keeps Kevin up at night? It's not the competition. 'We've had a great business model for 55 years and now how do we build on that foundation to do something that's both client driven and transformational? I know that this move is pertinent and will be relevant for the next 60 years. We can't keep ignoring new technologies that potentially disintermediate the lower end of our business.'

So far, this is confirmation of what we have already heard. This CEO, like others, knows that he has to take the first step towards transformational change. And he knows what needs to be done, even if he doesn't know how. Kevin adds: 'You have to drive significant change. There are tremendous opportunities that we can capture before our competitors.' And, under his leadership, Heidrick & Struggles has taken the first step. Kevin is stepping towards a future that he knows others cannot yet see, or believe.

When you are successful, it's so hard to see the need for change. If you are someone who can see ahead to an even brighter future, it's both a wonderful and a dangerous place to be. You could be taken for a visionary – or a foolish radical. So what's next?

Can you adapt to change?

Kevin offers some thoughtful advice.

'You have to take people with you. Darwin had it right, it's not the strongest or most intelligent who survive, it's those who adapt best to change. The Duke of Wellington had Lieutenant Atkinson as one of his best soldiers and the Battle of Waterloo was a decisive victory. The Duke acknowledged Atkinson's role, but also that he had his faults. He gets so far out in front of his men, sometimes they think he's the enemy.'

> if you get too far ahead, they won't go with you, and you'll be left stranded

This is such an adept analogy. So, it's your job to be out in front, taking the risky first step. We've already covered that. Here is the new idea. If you get too far ahead, they won't go with you, and you'll be left stranded. Look over your shoulder and you should see followers. If no-one's there, then you are not a leader – by definition.

Don't be a hot advocate

Any executive will tell you that some of the most dangerous people in any change agenda are the hot advocates. The ones who get the 'new world' fast and then surge ahead, trying to make it happen. And they scare people – away.[6] We all like to think we like change and we certainly are in favour of change that we start, that is, change that moves the way we think it should. We are never, ever, as human beings, as comfortable with other people's ideas about change. It's emotional. So in taking that first step, think ahead first. How are you going to get others to follow you? How will you make it seem less threatening, more achievable?

You know, there is a really interesting story at Ford that demonstrates what happens if you get too far ahead. Everyone knows that Bill Ford, great-grandson of Henry Ford, became CEO in October 2001, after their first outsider CEO, Jacques Nasser, was ousted. Nasser's departure reflected significant differences in corporate values – with Nasser focused on maximising corporate profits and shareholder value, while Ford was noted for valuing people and tradition. The company wanted to return to its core values and only a member of the Ford family could, in their minds, be trusted to do the job. So in 2001, Bill stepped forward into the CEO position. He was in the job for just under five years.[7]

On 5 September 2006, after a year of rumours that he 'wanted to spend more time with his family', Ford announced that he was stepping down as President and CEO, naming former Boeing senior executive Alan Mulally as his replacement. Ford continued as the company's Executive Chairman.

A hot advocate at Ford?

What about Bill Ford himself? How well did he really fit into the company that his great-grandfather founded? Bill is well known as a committed environmentalist and has published on the topic. So he is very keen to create fuel efficiency in a whole range of vehicles. In 2000, he announced that the company would achieve a 25 per cent improvement in fuel efficiency in the company's light truck fleet, including SUVs, by mid decade. That commitment proved to be impractical, given US consumer preference for heavy towing capacity and large, powerful engines in their trucks, so they never reached their goal. The Americans love their big cars and didn't want to give them up. Next, Ford terminated its electric vehicle programme as impractical and unaffordable from a profitable business standpoint.

Then, during 2006, there was an unexpectedly large swing in consumer demand away from pickups and SUVs to smaller cars and crossover vehicles. This was how the consumer chose to respond to higher fuel prices. Instead of opting for vehicles that could be as large, but powered in a different way, they chose to stick with fuel and save money through driving smaller vehicles. Given their move away from the alternative fuel agenda as a means of keeping large vehicles with lower fuel costs, Ford Motor Company was largely unprepared for such a sudden shift in demand. As a result, Ford's total market share dropped in the United States. Consumers saw lowered fuel consumption in smaller cars, rather than new technology, as the way to beat higher fuel prices.

Like his great-grandfather with his car for the masses, Bill Ford was ahead of his time. Under his direction, Ford made technological progress towards improving fuel efficiency, with the introduction of the Hybrid Electric Escape, one of the most fuel-efficient SUVs on the market. But consumers weren't ready to follow him – so maybe he was too far ahead? As Chairman, he is quoted as saying that he will not take up the CEO position again, but would rather 'spend his time focusing on the company's future than dealing with day-to-day concerns'.[8]

You can't separate this from self doubt

We have so far built a pretty impressive picture of leadership – of fearless and courageous leaders who see opportunities others don't, who push forwards and take big risks and rise above the criticism, however personal. So, never a moment's worry?

Quite the opposite. Having the courage to step into the unknown is not the same as placing a blind bet. So here is where we introduce self doubt as an important part of the package. Self doubt in this context doesn't mean that you are plagued by internal worries about your own capability. That kind of self doubt is disabling.

In this context, self doubt means that you don't always think you are 100 per cent right or have all the answers. It keeps you open to hearing the weak signals that may presage a radical change in your industry. It keeps you listening to outlandish ideas so that innovation stays alive and well in your organisation. And it helps you to identify where resistance lies among key stakeholders.

> self doubt means that you don't always think you are 100 per cent right or have all the answers

This can get scary

One leader in an interview was very clear about the need for self doubt. In his view, it's the way that we integrate outside perspectives to help us. This leader is also full of praise for the great leaders who have allowed him to learn from them, so he knows how to learn from others and to be open to different ways of thinking. He's not afraid of taking risks because he has learnt by working for someone who allowed him to make mistakes.

He recounted a story about a time in his life when he wanted to put forward a radical change in the industry he was then working in. It was the start of the 1980s and he was already holding down a big leadership role. He wanted to execute this change through buying two large companies in a different industry. It was a huge move, merging two industries, as big as the advent of broadband in the internet, so he had spent a lot of time preparing a detailed argument to put to the Board, with lots of supporting data. They were a tough crowd and he knew that this was an important moment.

Let's hear it in his own words. 'This can get scary. I stood quaking in front of the Board, at 39 years old, and the Chairman said "Stop; we put you in the job, it's your judgement call. The paper you are presenting is well thought out, but it will be irrelevant three months from now. Just don't screw it up.'" (By the way, in case you were wondering, this last comment was intended to be supportive and encouraging.)

Fear, self doubt, uncertainty. These are definitely not the adjectives we expect to see used to describe leaders. Yet there was this leader, already hugely successful at 39, quaking at the enormity of the decision he was presenting to the Board. Do you think they could see his nervousness? And he wasn't even allowed to finish his presentation. The Chairman said 'stop'. They knew that his carefully crafted words were logical, but it was action that mattered. When an industry is changing fast, you have to move at the same speed, or be left behind.

The other interesting piece in this story is that they were backing him as an individual, his instinct, his judgement in getting it right. The Board wasn't even all that interested in his well-researched presentation, because they knew how fast the industry was changing, so fast that his data would be irrelevant in three months' time. Quite simply, they trusted him.

What are his reflections now? They have the simplicity and directness you'd expect. 'When you wake up at 4 a.m., you don't take a pill or whine, you know how to make a judgement call.'

Lack of self doubt can bring you down

What happens if you lack self doubt – is it a problem?

If you believe the press reports about the former CEO of Nedbank, Richard Laubscher, who quit in 2003 after 10 years at the helm following an overpriced acquisition (some media reports at the time described him as a gambler), or the ones about Freddie Goodwin of RBS, it looks as though neither doubted their own strategy – and it ended in their downfall.

They are similar stories, but let's look at Sir Fred's in a little more detail. On 11 October 2008, Sir Fred officially announced his resignation as Chief Executive – a month before RBS announced that its 2008 loss totalled £24.1bn, the largest annual loss in UK corporate history at that time. He had grown RBS through an aggressive strategy of acquisition, but following investor unrest in the build-up to RBS's acquisition of a $1.6bn minority stake in Bank of China in 2005, Goodwin undertook to switch to organic growth.

He was criticised by some RBS shareholders for putting global expansion ahead of short-term financial returns and accused of megalomania by others, as reported by Dresdner Kleinwort analyst James Eden (who said he thought the label was 'unwarranted').[9]

In 2007, Goodwin went for another big acquisition, despite his earlier commitment to organic growth. He arranged a consortium of RBS, Fortis and former RBS shareholders Grupo Santander, to purchase the assets of ABN Amro and break them up in a three-way split. The deal was struck in October 2007 as the global liquidity crisis began to develop. Barclays withdrew its competing €61bn bid and ABN's shareholders endorsed the €71bn RBS takeover. The deal proved the final straw for RBS. According to the *Daily Mail*, Goodwin had been 'regarded by analysts as among the most arrogant figures in the City'.[10]

It's impossible to tell what really happened from the outside. All that can be said is that there is a fine line between the courage it takes to take the first step and, as one CEO put it, 'believing in your own press'. As a leader, if you have the courage to make the move, ensure that its companion is the courage to listen to divergent or opposing views without feeling threatened. Timing and luck will not always be on your side, but if important stakeholders believe that you have listened to them, then they will be more likely to understand the caprice of the markets. And they are likely to have some good ideas.

Beware arrogance

To be arrogant means to have or display an excessive sense of self-worth, self-importance or superiority. If you think you are better than others, then you're not going to be the greatest listener in the world, are you? Nor is it likely that there will be much room for self doubt. And it can get you into trouble. So it looks as though self doubt is an unlikely, but important, ingredient in *no safety net*. Without it, there can be significant consequences, not just for your career, but for your whole enterprise.

Are you brave enough to fail?

'You can tell an MBA anywhere, you just can't tell them anything.'[11] This gives the sense of MBAs being described as a smart elite who have never failed and so almost always think they are right. Of course it's not true, but it's funny because it contains a grain of truth. Some of these young people lead charmed lives. But lack of failure in your life can lead to complacency and an inflated sense of your own importance or invulnerability. On the other hand, it can also mean that you have never tried quite hard enough, never pushed beyond your comfort zone. In a way, you have stopped learning.

These leaders push the boundaries all the time. Sometimes the stakes are extraordinarily high.

Take for example the case of Kevin Sharer, the CEO of Amgen, a biotechnology company. Amgen is a Fortune 500 company, with sites from the US to Asia, which is dedicated to helping people fight serious illness through developing breakthrough medicines. Sharer spoke candidly about the risks he and the company took in developing denosumab, an osteoporosis drug. 'You only have to take a shot twice a year, and you're protected from osteoporosis. We're very, very excited about it. We're also developing it for a kind of bone cancer, and we look forward to the final results of those trials this year. This has been a drug we've worked on for 15 years. We did the fundamental biology and invested over \$1 billion. I bet my job on it. So I was happy that it turned out OK.'[12] From this quotation, it sounds as though CEO Kevin Sharer is willing to take big risks and is well aware of the consequences of failure.

The stakes are high and leaders love it – because if they succeed, they are out ahead of the pack. If you are afraid – of taking a risk, of losing your job, of damaging your reputation – it's unlikely that you will ever take the first step. And some people are afraid – too afraid to step forwards.

Is the public sector the same?

Let's turn now to a successful leader from a different kind of enterprise. Sir John Tusa has had a long career in the public sector. He is currently the Chairman of the University of the Arts, London. From 1980 to 1986 he was a main presenter of BBC 2's *Newsnight* programme and from 1986 to 1993 he was managing director of the BBC World Service. From 1995 until 2007 he was managing director of the City of London's Barbican Arts Centre. I know him from his time at the Barbican Centre, when I wrote a business school case study about leading change, using the Barbican as the example.

John is a well-known figure and still active in broadcasting. From October 2009 until the end of the year he presented a 91-part series on BBC Radio 4. The series was called *Day by Day* and used original archive news material to track events on a daily basis from 1989, including the fall of the Berlin Wall. He has strong views and is not afraid to express them. For example, since leaving his BBC World Service post, John has been critical of some BBC policies, including the former director general John Birt's management style and decisions to pare down World Service activities in Europe. Fear of failure, or any other kind, doesn't seem to appear in Sir John's vocabulary.

Uncharted waters

John reflects on his career. 'Often there is no safety net because you are moving the organisation into uncharted waters and I have a history of doing this. In political situations, you can choose to speak up or to toe the government line. Lots of people don't want to pick a fight, but you have to, especially on matters that are important. I took on the Arts Council when at the Barbican and the Foreign Office when at the World Service. I was told that the FO was quite frightened of me, so in that situation, I took a lot of risks. Today people are telling me that I can't take on the government and my response is "or else what?"'

What do we hear? Again there is that thread of certainty and conviction when faced with a large and complex challenge. But this insight takes it one step further. It's about being willing to take the fight even to much bigger institutions than your own. It's to look across the abyss and say 'so what?' It's to be outside your comfort zone and well into the arena where failure is a possibility.

Not 100 per cent right

Time and again CEOs say 'I am not 100 per cent right all the time.' This is a huge difference for today's leaders. Fifty years ago there was an apocryphal saying that 'getting to the top means never being told I am wrong ever again'. You can still see this syndrome sometimes where a successful CEO has been in position for a while, say 10 years or more (the average CEO tenure in 2010 is 6.6 years[13]).

The longer a CEO is in charge, the more of a halo effect grows up around him or her, and they come to be seen as invincible. As the gap between the CEO and potential successors widens, dependency grows and the organisation grows fearful of what will happen should the CEO ever leave. It is always hard for a CEO to get hold of bad news (getting good news is not a challenge) and so to be realistic about the organisation's position as well as their own personal situation. In cases of long tenure it becomes even harder to get hold of the truth. One Canadian CEO, so the story goes, was told 'the day you became CEO was the last day you will ever be told the truth'.

Accept that, despite experience, skill and a good intuition, sometimes you will make mistakes, you will not get it right. Can you welcome this, rather than avoid it? It will make you more approachable, you will be more likely to receive candid analysis and it will, by example, give others permission to fail too. This is definitely a way of thinking that some will find too challenging. Are you one of them? How great a premium do you place on being right?

What happens if you don't get your thinking right?

The stories you have read in this chapter about Ford and about RBS show that, because you run the shop, if you misstep it's likely that the whole organisation will too. You will hear this refrain in every chapter. There will always be personal consequences. There will also be organisational consequences. Sometimes their magnitude will not match.

No safety net takes courage. And without thinking like this, you can stop your career in its tracks. As one CEO said, 'Who doesn't make it? Those who don't show courage, who don't own something big, or go out on a limb, or move it forward.'

Another saying people love to use about running big organisations is that there is 'a safe pair of hands' at the top. This brings a feeling of reassurance. Yet when we look at the big 'misses', it is often precisely because the pair of hands at the top is too safe. Could almost be called risk averse. Or prone to too much analysis. Either way, decisions aren't taken and you get stuck.

It's bad for the organisation. It means that opportunities are not grasped and, while you cling onto the safety net, others step forwards and you become irrelevant. It can happen fast. For example, 10 years ago which company would you have guessed as being the largest distributor of music in the world in 2010? (Except for Steve Jobs, no one would have guessed Apple.) Who, given their technical capabilities and talent management, should have come up with the 'iPod' type of device? (Sony had the technology and the content – not Apple.)

Who would have guessed 10 years ago that the most movies rented in 2010 would be delivered by NetFlix? (Not Blockbuster, which was the market leader in 2000.) These are a couple of examples of 'burning opportunities' that were seized by companies outside an industry, while the incumbents sat and watched in disbelief.

A final thought

Let's close by introducing briefly just one more CEO. Irene Dorner is the US CEO for HSBC. The United States must undoubtedly be one of the most challenging places in the world to run a bank in 2010. Irene is a big character – she has to be, as she is one of the very few women at the top. She is an absolute straight talker, dynamic and exuberant. She takes her personal leadership extremely seriously. She pays attention to it, she listens to feedback, she decides if it is good advice or not, and if it is, she acts on it. Irene and I have been bumping into each other for about 10 years now, on a variety of ventures in different places around the world. She's incredibly busy and very devoted to her career. I have probably spent more time keeping in touch with her husband via email, as they move around the world, than I have with her.

Irene says: 'I think about my job ALL the time, but I am a free spirit and don't owe my soul to this bank. I care passionately about what I do, but I am less frightened and less co-dependent than others. I don't need to be liked. A lot of people are gifted like me, but don't feel their freedom. You need to be self sufficient, self driven and know what you need. I am willing to argue back. Learning to operate without a safety net – previously I took the strategy and implemented it, worked for a boss. Now I make it, live it, deliver it; the buck stops here. You have to consciously think: 'I know I can do this.' The position is incredibly lonely; you need enormous strength of character. No-one explains that doing what you are told is not enough; you have to be more than a good soldier.'

What a great summary of what *no safety net* is all about. With this way of thinking you are ultimately accountable, not for the status quo, but for change. You have the courage to step into the unknown, to lead the way. And you have the resilience to repeat this, time and time again. You are willing to lean into unknown risk.

This doesn't mean you don't take advice; the opposite is true. Every story tells the importance of counsel; from the senior team, from the chairman, from a mentor. The peers and advisors can advise, but you push the boundaries and it is you who takes the decision. Ultimately no-one can provide reassurance on the risks that you take. You are the one pushing forwards, understanding the opportunity to be had in uncharted waters. More than courage, it is fearlessness and the determination to do what matters, what must be done. And failure can happen, but it doesn't daunt you.

Developing *no safety net* thinking: self assessment

What is at the heart of *no safety net*? Consider the following questions:

- Do you understand that you are alone? Are you willing to be the one to stand up and take the difficult decision? Do you understand that you are paid to take the big risks?

- Have you got the courage to take the first step? Do you realise that nothing will happen until you move? Can you take the first step without thought for your personal consequences?

- Can you ensure you won't get so far ahead that you look like the enemy? Can you take people with you? Will they trust you?

▌ Can you keep a good healthy dose of self doubt? Can you keep listening despite the tumult you create by moving the enterprise? Can you keep an open mind while looking confident to others?

▌ Are you brave enough to fail? Do you have the courage to accept the stigma of failure? Are you resilient enough to try again?

You are fearless and determined; you can take the organisation out to the edge; you make ground-breaking moves and decisions; and you move the enterprise forward, into uncharted territory.

chapter

3

Comfortable in discomfort

D r Arthur Jensen is a Professor Emeritus of educational psychology at the University of California, Berkeley. You become an Emeritus Professor if you have contributed so much intellectual capital to your research area that they never want you to retire. It's like having a permanent key to the boardroom. Dr Jensen is a somewhat controversial figure (he believes that genetics trump nurture in how we end up as human beings) and has published over 400 scientific papers. In 1981, he published a book setting out his research showing that executives tend to have an IQ of 125 or above, putting them in the top 3 per cent of the population.[14]

You are in this band.

You are decisive. You have a capacity for data and synthesis. You can hold a lot of information in your head and analyse it to draw conclusions. You may even have an MBA degree, in which case you have certainly learnt the black art of 'scientific' analysis. You can crunch the data, find the flaws and make the call. And if there isn't enough data, you have learnt the hard way to hold out for more. Sometimes, you feel it's too early to decide and so you set about gathering more information for dissection. You are looking for patterns and trends that give a hint to the future and you are good at it. Not everyone can see 'the matrix', the themes inside the data, but you can. You have the horsepower.

This chapter introduces the second way of thinking, a new trick. To have the courage to take the decision when you don't have all the information, when you are struggling to find the answer but you know that you have to move – now. And to live with the discomfort it brings, the uncertainty, the nervousness, the tension. And not to mind. Think *comfortable in discomfort.* This story describes it.

Meeting the CEO

The room is packed and it's hot. People at the back open the door to let in the cool night air and the exotic sounds of the African evening seep in alongside. Nothing breaks the concentration in the room. For some, it's the first time that they have met their CEO and they are intent on understanding more about the strategy and their role in it.

They are also intent on understanding more about him. The company has global ambitions and has been expanding internationally through acquisitions, throughout Africa, but also as far afield as Argentina. These executives want to see if their CEO has the mettle to lead them. You can hear it in their questions. Some are thinking 'what does a South African know about Argentina?'

Ambitions for expansion

Jacko Maree, the Group CEO of Standard Bank, has been CEO for over 10 years and is highly regarded in South Africa, both within and outside the bank. Why? Because he takes his role in helping to build South Africa as a nation seriously and he is successfully taking Standard Bank global. Both of these help to put South Africa on the map.

Jacko's current strategy is to move from a comfortable and successful South African bank, to leading a complex organisation that spans the Urals to the Andes. As we heard briefly in Chapter 2, his bank is also one of the early adopters of the accelerating South–South connection. This is the growing trade and partnership between companies based in the Southern Hemisphere, for example between Africa and China. The largest deal in South Africa was when the Industrial and Commercial Bank of China (ICBC) paid 5.5 billion Rand for a 20 per cent stake in Standard Bank in 2008.

The deals being struck are big. In June 2010 the Chinese state firm Jinchuan invested almost 900 million Rand in the platinum industry through a 51 per cent stake in Wesizwe. Standard Bank, South Africa's largest bank by assets in 2010, is at the head of this wave and reaping the commercial benefits. In August 2010, the bank signed two agreements to be financial advisor to two giant Chinese companies, the China Railway Group and Guangdong Power Company. Jacko says: 'There has been no question that we have now a completely different interface with China than we had before. For us, the immediate short-term opportunity is to help Chinese companies, most of whom are developing some kind of Africa strategy.'[15]

This series of 'firsts' has taken Jacko Maree well into the discomfort zone.

Like many other CEOs, his intellect distinguishes him, but more than that, he is quite simply a happy man. He has a healthy, rosy complexion and he smiles most of the time. He loves engaging in debate and he has a clear and certain view of the world that he communicates easily. He is dedicated to Standard Bank and employees respect him. Jacko answers question after question; he is relaxed, warm and affable, but you can hear the sharp intellect that whirrs just underneath. Over 10 years as CEO has given him plenty of practice with these events.

The diversity in the room is unexpected at this senior level, where often organisations find the room full of executives that represent only the country of origin.[16] Here we have South

Africans, Argentinians, Russians, English and Nigerians among others. The questions probe thick and fast: why this investment, why that move, what did that decision mean? It's not just that he's comfortable under this quickfire onslaught; this is how he thinks about the business.

I recall his words from one of our many conversations over three years of working together. 'Often I don't know where I am going. Being comfortable in discomfort is a critical dimension for a leader. There is lots of grey, lots of ways to solve a problem, often no one way is right. You live with the problem for a while. Most people can't deal with this, they are always looking for THE answer. You are checking your gut feel, if it fits with the company, getting other inputs. You need self-confidence to be comfortable here. I was a mathematician. This has come to me with maturity.'

What is *comfortable in discomfort*?

Let's unpeel some of the layers here. Jacko thinks being comfortable in discomfort is a critical dimension for a leader, so that's a big tick for the concept itself. He is also, unknowingly, laying out some of its foundations that are found in more detail in this chapter. He tells us that he doesn't always know where he is going and he has to live with the uncertainty. How does that sit with the leader's job of having a vision and giving the organisation direction? Especially if he's right and most people can't live with the uncertainty, they need to hear the answer (from him) straight away. He thinks that there's lots of grey and not one right answer.

Jacko's first degree was in economics, accountancy and mathematics. So he explains that he has grown into this way of thinking over the years. You can imagine that a young mathematician might not have been so comfortable with the possibility of multiple potential answers. That's a big shift in thinking. And what's he doing while he's living with the uncertainty? He's checking out the feel of the thing. Not the facts, not the data, but the feel. How well does it sit with his instincts? What do others think? Does it work with the way the organisation does business now, or should it change its approach?

The metaphor is a traveller

If you think about it, it's a bit like being a traveller. You have a destination in mind, but you're not quite sure what it is like or how the journey will be. Sometimes the bed (or the campsite, or plane) isn't as comfortable as you might have expected – but it's an adventure, so you live with it. And the more you travel, just like Jacko, the more comfortable you get with the unexpected.

Books on management will tell you that managers are paid to take decisions.[17] Early in their careers, they are rewarded for crunching the data, analysing the pros and cons, presenting the case and making the call. Yes or no. In fact, most MBA courses emphasise the importance of decisiveness (they even have courses on decision theory). If you can't decide, you are deemed to suffer from 'analysis paralysis' – and that is seen as a disadvantage.

What we hear from Jacko is that leaders are sometimes paid for the opposite; not deciding immediately, so they may delay a decision even though, on the face of it, there is enough data to decide. It's not analysis paralysis – they could call it, but they consciously take the decision to delay. Something about the timing just doesn't feel right, or maybe stakeholders haven't had a chance to buy in, or they sense something else in the wind that has to be allowed to play itself out first. And they can withstand the pressure to move to a conclusion.

Interestingly, this way of thinking is also about the opposite. It's also about being able to decide despite there being insufficient data to make the decision clear cut.

As executives become more senior the decisions get bigger and more complex. Sometimes there is insufficient information, but if you wait until you have all the data the decision will never be made. Globalisation has brought with it giant organisations that outrank small and medium-sized national governments in revenue and power. The way forwards is often unclear and strategic thinking, which we should re-title 'the ability to peer through fog', has replaced strategic planning, because there are just too many variables in play.

> if you wait until you have all the data the decision will never be made

Leaders are paid to make judgements

Managers are paid to take decisions. Leaders are paid to make judgements. Can you hold the tension?

There are five aspects to *comfortable in discomfort.*

The first is that, as a leader, sometimes you will have to operate in a grey area, where you may not have all the data you need to take a decision. It's about instinct and speed – but it's not about assuming that the future will be the same as the past.

Second, you need to learn to love ambiguity – today we live in a 'yes, and' world, rather than an 'either-or' world.

The third idea is that, paradoxically, sometimes it's about delaying a decision – keeping an open mind. Whether you have enough data or not, the timing of the decision has to be right and sometimes this means keeping a decision open, even when others are urging you to decide.

Fourth, you need to be comfortable with surprising people from time to time – you won't always be predictable.

And lastly, despite all the uncertainty, you have to be able to explain your decisions in a way that makes sense to others, even though the logic may not even be clear to you. Your followers need a sense of direction and purpose.

Let's start with what it feels like to take decisions when you know you don't have as many facts as you would like.

Living with grey

Let's check back in with our former CEO and now seasoned Chairman, Dennis Nally, from Chapter 1. What does he think about the role of facts in decision-making at the top? 'Today, you make a left turn, a right turn, you don't know the route, but I have to take a decision or I will fall behind. I am not 100 per cent right all the time. Often you can't take the time to do all the analysis. You can be informed and thoughtful but you don't have all the facts. This puts risk into the thought process. You can analyse nine ways to Sunday, but you don't have time and the world is too complicated.'

You may not have all the facts

Think about what Dennis just said. The first proposition is that you may not have all the facts. Imagine the situation where you decide to set up in, well, let's stick with China, for the first time. You can scope the decision so that you reduce the uncertainty as much as possible. You can buy market data reports, you can hire locals with special insight, you can run trials, but you will never have all the information you need. Let's take a real example. More than one company trying to enter China has found that litigation becomes part of doing business there – but if you win the court battle you can lose the market war. What does this mean? If the court finds in your favour, the government is then, paradoxically for a Western mind, likely to be even stricter in its dealings with you to avoid any stigma of favouritism. This is not something you can predict or build into a decision tree. It's unexpected, counter-intuitive and real in its impact.

The Rio Tinto story

Tom Albanese became CEO of the mining giant Rio Tinto in May 2007. In his short, but turbulent, time as CEO, he has often found himself in a situation where he did not have all the facts. Founded in 1873, Rio Tinto is now one of the four largest mining companies in the world. Tom's first three years as CEO were eventful, to say the least. Within a month of taking the job, he started the process of acquiring Alcan, the Canadian aluminium company as big as Rio Tinto itself at that time. As the world moved into recession, streamlining the assets of the co-joined companies to reduce debt became a priority. (In the commodities business, any downturn has immediate impact – business falls off the cliff.) BHP Billiton then launched a hostile takeover, a campaign that would last an exhausting year before being dropped towards the end of 2008. In 2009, the Chinese government-owned resources group Chinalco (already a major shareholder in Rio Tinto) started talks to take a bigger stake. In the same year, four Rio Tinto employees were arrested in Shanghai accused of corruption and espionage. In terms of CEO induction, this has to rank as one of the most challenging series of events – a CEO boot camp.

As we build up a picture of the character of the leader, it is unsurprising to note that Tom is dedicated to Rio Tinto and, luckily for him, an optimist with a sound constitution. How else would he deal with such enormous levels of uncertainty with equanimity? He comments: 'The toughest decisions are where you have the least amount of data. For example, the decision to get closer to China as a strategic relationship – you can't put that on a spreadsheet.' So he makes the point that, in big strategic decisions, there are some investments to be made that are unquantifiable.

Tom continues: 'We muddle accuracy and precision; accuracy is getting the right answer, precision is getting the numbers in the cash flow model right, to the decimal point. The system drives towards precision, but from the CEO perspective, the information only gets you to solve one part of the puzzle.' This is a very helpful distinction. Don't confuse figures (which can be calculated with apparent accuracy) with the right answer. There is broader information to be taken into account. If you let the data that you can collect drive the decision, you may end up driving in the wrong direction.

You can't wait

Back to Dennis Nally. His second proposition is that, even if you could get hold of all the data, you just don't have the time. The world is moving too fast to wait for you to get comfortable. Don't sit and wait while others overtake you, live with the discomfort and make the call.

Sometimes executives cling to the data because it gives them comfort. In an uncertain world, it adds up, when nothing else may do. Here's an example. In a meeting with the executive group of a multinational company in the late 1990s, I heard that their economic performance compared with their global competition was dire. Their return on investment was running at about 19 per cent compared with the competition's 30 to 35 per cent range. We were trying to help them see the disparity, to create the legendary 'burning platform for change'. They didn't even believe that the platform was smouldering. The executives fixated on the analysis of 19 per cent and spent a large part of the meeting arguing about whether, in fact, it should be 20 per cent. They were clinging myopically to unreality and were frozen into inaction. The following year, their industry ranking plummeted – it was a dramatic fall. Only in crisis were they goaded into action.

Dennis's third proposition echoes Jacko Maree's. You may not know where you are going, or even if you do know where you are going, you don't know how to get there. You don't know where and you don't know how, but you have an instinct around 'what'. This was a theme that was repeated by the leaders over and over again.

It's about instinct

One leader had a particularly forthright view about the usefulness of facts in big, complex, strategic decisions. For this individual, while it's about balanced risk, it's also about instinct – and instinct that builds the business for the long run, not the short haul. 'It's not about a 22 per cent internal rate of return, that may get you through to the next quarter, or even the quarter after, but then you are gone. You have to build the business for the longer term, not just rely on measuring short-term results, or you will be caught out by the business cycle. You have to recognise that there is no truth or objectivity in what you do as a manager. Sometimes if the data tells you it's 49/51, screw it, we'll take the 49!'

The past is not a good predictor of the future

It's time to meet another leader. We came across Paul Thurston briefly in Chapter 2. Paul is a Group Managing Director with the HSBC banking Group, and Chief Executive, HSBC Retail Banking and Wealth Management. Paul has responsibility for HSBC's consumer and commercial banking businesses in the UK. He has 35 years' experience in the banking industry with the HSBC Group, both in the UK and around the world. He is known for three things: strategic leadership; getting (big) stuff done; and a passion for developing people. He has absolute strategic clarity. He can step back and look at the business and know what it needs. And for him, developing people to enable them to move the business forward is top and centre of his agenda. He is masterful at gaining buy-in through the way he engages with people.

'You have to be comfortable operating in discomfort. Most of the decisions that I make are in areas of uncertainty that don't have easily discernible, guaranteed, right or wrong answers. You won't find answers in policies or rule books. If it were that easy someone else would already have made the decision. And in a changing world, the past is not always a good predictor of the future, so you can't simply rely on historical evidence.'

We hear a similar but different theme. Paul is counselling against building a picture of the future based on what has happened in the past. He almost seems to be telling us to expect the unexpected. So in the absence of data, don't be tempted to expect a straight line move from where you are today. It might make you comfortable, but it's unlikely to keep you successful. And again there is that refrain about not necessarily knowing where you are going, uncertainty about how you are going to get there – but knowing what the enterprise needs to be.

> don't be tempted to expect a straight line move from where you are today

Think about your own leadership for a moment. Do you find yourself extrapolating next year's revenue from this year's figures? Is what you call strategic planning more like budgeting in reality? Do you spend time thinking about what your organisation needs to become, rather than extending current reality into the future? Can you learn to love ambiguity?

Learn to love ambiguity

'We are good at execution, but we are not good enough in dealing with super flux.' This quote from a Group Head of Human Resources says it all. She was commenting on the need to develop the talent in her organisation to be better at dealing with the huge amounts of change hitting the business. Today's world is about major and unexpected shifts in the tectonic plates of business. We need to be able to keep our balance and to stay upright.

In the previous section we talked about letting go of the spurious comfort that data can provide. Data can lock you into complacency – 'we're no worse than anyone else'. Facts can give you a false sense of security. While the game changes around you, if you continue to measure your success by looking at the old way of doing business, you will eventually fail. There is also a personal side to this. You personally need to be able to live with the ambiguity.

One CEO talked about living not just with grey, but with shades of grey. In addition, he offered this advice. 'Live with shades of grey successfully and you move up higher than those who can't. There is greater ambiguity the higher up the chain you go, it can be 51/49, so data alone doesn't decide. You take the decision and there is tension in it that you have to absorb and can't pass on. Eat the uncertainty.'

The discomfort stops with you

What does this advice tell us? We hear the familiar theme of insufficient facts, but we also hear the idea that personal success can depend upon how well we can live with the discomfort that uncertainty brings. And there's more. The counsel is to 'eat the uncertainty'. That means that the ambiguity and uncertainty sit inside you and that you don't pass them on. You live with the ambiguity and any tension you feel doesn't transmit itself to others. For the people who follow you, you look comfortable in the situation and so they in turn feel comfortable to follow you. Coping with the ambiguity is one thing, but wouldn't it be great if you could actually relish and enjoy it?

It's worth pausing here to ask yourself a few more questions.

▌ How well do you cope with ambiguous situations?

▌ Can you tolerate the tension and uncertainty that comes with situations that span shades of grey?

▌ Do you value control too much to be able to be flexible?

▌ Can you see that, as a leader of leaders, you are out of control, while in command?

It's a 'yes, and' world

It has been unfashionable recently to talk about the intellectual horsepower it takes to lead an enterprise, but it is clear that you have to be pretty smart to handle the complexity of the job, especially in a global context. Recall from the start of this chapter that executives in general have well above average IQs (getting up to around 135 for the chief executive) and so have a huge capacity for analysis. You need to deal with large amounts of data and competing concepts. You have to be able to hold two opposing ideas in your head at the same time. Gone are the days where you could solve a problem for a single 'answer' – as a leader, you are continually faced with 'and' issues that you have to work through. You know many of these well, for example, profit *and* growth; short-term quarterly results *and* long-term investment. The simple truth is that you have to handle an increasing amount of cognitive complexity.

As the leader, you execute very little; others do that for you. You can only guide and hope to do so in a way that makes it work. And you have to live with the resulting ambiguity.

> as the leader, you execute very little; others do that for you

Encourage from the sidelines

One CEO, who has run countries and territories for a technology company all over the world, explained how he settled the question for himself. 'I am more strategic myself now and coach my people to execute like I used to. The paradox is that the more senior I become, the more I step out rather than step in. If I step in I will be a block; operating from the edge I am a catalyst and must ask the right questions.'

Let's be clear about what he is saying. The more senior you become, the more you rely on others to execute. This is a big step into uncertainty. Rather than acting yourself (and your track record shows that you are good at getting stuff done), you have to make space for others to execute on your behalf. Your role moves from the comfort of doing a good job yourself, to encouraging and steering the action from the sidelines. You are accountable for more, but in control of less. It's a bit like being a basketball coach. You are committed to winning and you give it your all – but you don't get to touch the ball once.

Can you learn it?

Suppose you are high on control and like structure more than free flow. Can you change and learn to become more comfortable with ambiguity? Jasmine Whitbread from Save the Children thinks so. 'I talk of the years I spent at Thompson as formative in my career. My boss was like that; in technology, we made it up as we went along. I feel fortunate because I am comfortable in uncertainty and was allowed to welcome ambiguity – this can be taught and facilitated.'

The point she's making is that you can learn to be more comfortable with ambiguity and that a good boss, who gives you leeway, can help.[18] So if you don't feel so comfortable here, think how you can develop this further. Can your boss help? And as a boss yourself, how can you help others to be more at ease with uncertainty?

Don't close down too early

So far the idea has been about reaching a judgement without definitive support from the data and then living with the uncertainty this creates. As one Chairman put it, 'If the data is so smart, it can have the seat on the Board!'

But sometimes it's about NOT deciding. Let's reflect on something that Jacko Maree said earlier. 'You live with the problem for a while. Most people can't deal with this, they are always looking for THE answer.'

One refrain over the years, in hours and hours of classroom discussion, has been about this tension. Mid-level executives will exclaim 'Why can't they just tell us where we are going and what we need to do! Then we would be able to get on and execute against it.' 'They' in this sentence means the CEO and the Executive Committee. Very senior executives have a slightly different refrain, about the same 'they'. 'Why can't they just be clearer about the strategy?' Why, indeed?

It's very complicated

Imagine yourself in the following situation. This is a real, but disguised situation (and it's not the Standard Bank story). As business moves east, you have decided to invest in China. This is the coming trend. Before the 2008 global recession, the emerging economies were growing much faster than the developed ones and in 2010, they were recovering faster. The business proposition is attractive. Your executives now understand that investing in China is part of the company's core strategy. It will not be clear to them exactly what this means or how it will be achieved.

You have decided that the best way to be welcomed into the market is to accept a large shareholding from a Chinese company. This will give you superior access to limited local resources in China and access to opportunities not afforded to other foreign companies. Your Western shareholders are anxious about this investment, because they see it diluting the value of their shareholding and are also worried about what it means for how the company will be run in the future.

You have the opportunity to invest in a big project jointly with your Chinese investor, but you are uncertain whether this is a good idea. This has to be handled delicately, because the Chinese do not want to lose face. Meanwhile, the government in your home country starts threatening to pass legislation, because they don't want to 'lose' you to China. At the same time, you can see parallel opportunities for a big joint deal with one of your biggest competitors. You can probably handle the complexity of one complicated deal, but maybe not both at the same time. What should you do?

The timing has to be right

Well, what you shouldn't do is rush to close any decision! Maybe the deals can be achieved in parallel, or maybe one has to be chosen over another. There are big stakes for both governments involved and you have to work out how they might react to either or both deals. You also know that your phone is being tapped and so you have to be very cautious. There are delicate private and public negotiations to be done. This is the real world of uncertainty that CEOs inhabit. Being decisive is still a good thing – just not always immediately. You have to get the timing right.

People decisions are the hardest

Let's take another example where the stakes are equally high, but it's a people decision that is at stake. These are some of the most difficult decisions[19] that CEOs grapple with – who to keep on the team, who doesn't fit, the most likely successors and how to develop them. It's not just a question of scarce talent, although that features prominently. It's also that the talent may or may not be loyal, may have specific foibles that need attention, and will almost certainly have strong views about what they will and won't do.

In conversation with one leader, it was apparent that he had in mind a slot that he considered a promotion and a big signal to the organisation. The individual he wanted to move had a different view – he had to be persuaded to take it. It's a difficult juggling act.

In this new scenario, as CEO you want to undertake a major restructuring of the business. This will not only signal to the markets and to your employees that you are moving from a regional to a global player, it will also turn the business model on its head. You need to persuade one very senior executive to take on a new global role. The challenge is that your executive is suspicious about the move. He sees it as a lateral move, while you believe that it is a step up. It puts him in a different relationship with his peers, who also have to be persuaded to see this as an important move, not a sideways step. The reality is that, if this executive performs well in the global role, he will slowly rise to become more important than his regional peers. A further complication is that his successor is not completely ready to take over. More than that, the Group CEO needs to buy into the restructuring and a whole slew of company policies need to change to match the emerging global model.

There are lots of stakeholders

What does our executive say? 'I go into it with a bit of angst. This is a game-changing move for us.' It's also one that doesn't happen fast. Many stakeholders need to buy into the decision in parallel. Although the CEO may have a plan, he is ready to flex it if something unexpected happens. He is not closing down or announcing the central decision until he has positioned the move for success.

Can you think about what this means for you? You have a favoured route you see ahead, but you can't close down on the options. If you do, you could offend key stakeholders or lose key constituents. It's like a good game of chess – you can't move too early. Can you live with an open-ended situation, or do you find yourself moving to close down the uncertainty? As Jacko challenges us, can you live with the problem for a while?

can you live with the problem for a while?

So far, we have looked at three aspects of *comfortable in discomfort*. As a leader, you need to live with grey and shades of grey, because in big, complex decisions, it's highly unlikely that you will be able to get hold of all the information that you need. You need to be comfortable with ambiguity because it's a mistake to pass on any of the tension you may be feeling while you delay. Followers need to feel sure that you are delaying for a reason, not prevaricating. And you have to get the timing right. Sometimes you don't want to decide, even if you have all the information that you need, because you sense that it's the wrong time to make a move.

The next section is very new. Leaders get a lot of advice about being clear and over-communicating to get their point across. Sometimes, it's about the opposite – it's about surprising people. It's about not being predictable.

The power of surprise

Let's pause and think about how this must feel to followers. Few people have the confidence to 'eat the uncertainty' and not to pass the tension on to others. The leaders we admire seem to be at ease with the job, however big and challenging. When we are uncertain, they are available for a conversation, or to take part in a town hall meeting or a video conference to reassure us. We follow them because they seem to know what they are doing and we think they are good at the job. We listen carefully to their messages, watch their behaviour and gain assurance from this. We form a view of where we are headed next. So a big part of their job is about reassurance and giving followers certainty.

But that's only part of the story.

Be unexpected

Paul Thurston has a view on this. 'Part of leadership is being consistent but retaining the ability to come out with the unexpected at the same time. It's about the power of surprise. True leaders will take the conversation in a different direction – to take us to a new level – we got here, so now we are moving on. They constantly take you forwards. They are never satisfied with themselves – you can't read or anticipate them.'

So being comfortable with discomfort also means being ready to make the unexpected move, a lateral arabesque that no-one expects.

As you hold the tension and live with the grey, as you pause before you decide – suddenly a new opportunity presents itself. Or you see a different combination of events that could move you in an unexpected direction. And you are happy to go there. To the rest of the world, it can feel like a surprise. The whole idea of a strategy that gets you from A to B is turned on its head, as the strategy may get you from A to L instead, with a curve back to D.

A lateral arabesque[20]

In Chapter 6 we will hear Richard Fleck's story – this is by way of a prequel. Richard was, until 2005, a lead partner at Herbert Smith, the law firm. He is widely credited with taking Herbert Smith international, from a strong UK base. He has surprised people throughout his career, from proposing counter-intuitive strategic moves (going into Russia in 1998, just as everyone else was leaving) to unexpected manoeuvres in litigation. One partner practically exploded with frustration when he pulled off a coup that she had not foreseen despite many hours of preparation. On another occasion, his whole litigation team (including Counsel) signed a letter advising him that it would be negligent if he didn't adopt a particular legal tactic – he didn't and the result was an amazing legal victory. People don't get so surprised or indignant today when Richard makes a counter-intuitive move, because they know it is likely to be successful.

Richard says: 'This comes from totally immersing yourself in a situation, so that your antennae can pick up things that logical analysis doesn't expose. I will never do an important negotiation by video, because I want to be able to pick up intangible facets through the dynamics in the room.'

'If you are genuinely leading, you are by definition on an uncertain journey. As a leader you cannot worry about doing what everybody else is doing. That is not leadership, that is a herd mentality.'

Richard is attributing his capacity to surprise people, to take the unexpected direction, to a deep intuition grounded in immersion – essentially doing lots of homework and then carefully observing the dynamics in the room. And to not worrying about adopting a different point of view – as a leader, his view is that you should expect your ideas to be different and unusual.

It's not about poor communications

The lateral arabesque has to be intentional. The power of surprise should feel to followers like an unexpected yet interesting proposition that they had not foreseen. A creative opportunity that they had not spotted. It should not be the result of poor communication. One CEO said: 'I was warned that I am cleverer than most people and I go straight to the conclusion without walking people through it stepwise, so I come across as arrogant.' There then followed a story about how you can't act in this way even with your peers, because they also need to follow you and support you as you take on the unknown.

But the point is clear. This is not about being a poor communicator – after all, you need them to come with you. Instead, it's a bit like reading the tea leaves in the bottom of a cup (or maybe the grounds of coffee) and seeing a different picture than most others can see. And it's about doing this on a regular basis. As Paul says, good leaders constantly move you forwards. Just at the point when everyone else is just getting to grips with something new, they are ready to move on again.

> good leaders see a different picture than most others can see

Are we talking about creativity here? Maybe. Or perhaps it's experience, or the ability to see emergent themes or read weak signals. Maybe it's a combination of all of them. What we know is that the underpinning is how you think. If you are comfortable in discomfort, you will not always be predictable, because you will be comfortable in embracing the unexpected.

The final aspect to this way of thinking is about trying to signal the future direction, even when it is grey and unclear.

The vision thing

This wouldn't be a book on leadership if it didn't contain this word, would it?

We know that leaders hold up a vision to give a sense of direction, to seek alignment and to stop daily squabbles by providing a goal that is bigger than individual concerns. The paradox here is that you still have to hold up a vision, even if you don't know exactly where you're going. But think about it.

Isn't one of the reasons that executives complain about lack of clarity in the strategy that the CEO is not always sure what is coming next? And only the good ones can make apparent order appear out of chaos.

Let's take an example. Here is Paul Thurston again: 'You have to be comfortable dealing with a lot of the unknown yourself and at the same time be able to provide coherent leadership to your business and all of its stakeholders. Having a clear vision enables you to engage your stakeholders in that vision and helps you to gain support for the decisions you make along the way. You have to have clarity of vision for the enterprise.'

This is complicated, so let's be clear what Paul is saying. As a leader, you face a lot of uncertainty. You also have to manage the many and divergent views of a variety of stakeholders. A stakeholder is literally anyone who has a stake, or interest, in the outcome of your work. For a business, typical stakeholders among others would be shareholders, employees and local communities where you are based.[21] For a charity, they might be volunteers, the individuals or organisations that the charity supports and employees. These stakeholders will all have an opinion about how you are organised and what you do. And it is unlikely that they will agree amongst themselves what this should look like.

Despite the fact that you are trying to move forwards, but not always sure exactly where, and despite the fact that your stakeholders want different things from you, you still need to compile a credible and coherent story about where you are headed. You need to hold up an exciting picture of the future to engage others along the way.

A 102-year vision

The Alibaba Group, an e-commerce company that has its own version of an online payment system, is now larger than PayPal in terms of global users. It was started in 1999, established by

18 founders, led by Jack Ma (now Chairman and CEO) working out of an apartment in Hangzhou, in the Yangtze River Delta and just over 100 miles from Shanghai. It now has 18,000 employees in more than 50 cities throughout the world.

Alibaba's operations include Taobao, the largest online retail site in China with 82 per cent of the domestic online consumer market; Alipay, China's leading online payment platform; Alibaba Cloud Computing; and China Yahoo, acquired in October 2005 in a strategic deal with Yahoo!.

Alibaba.com remains the founding star of the Alibaba Group. It is built around three marketplaces: a global trade marketplace for importers and exporters, a marketplace for domestic trade in China and a Japanese marketplace. These marketplaces have more than 47 million registered users drawn from over 240 countries. Alibaba.com was floated on the Hong Kong Stock Exchange in 2007. Its initial public offering was worth $1.7 billion and it was the biggest Internet IPO since Google's arrival on the NASDAQ in 2004.

David Wei became Alibaba.com's chief executive in October 2007 after joining the Alibaba Group a year earlier. He is robust about the importance of holding up a 102-year vision for the Group. 'We really truly believe [in the timeline], and we count how many years we have to survive,' he says. 'For Alibaba, it's a vision-driven strategy. It's what happens in 5 years' time or 10 years' time. That's all we think about.'

Leadership is full of paradoxes. This one requires the leader to hold up a coherent picture of the future, when it isn't clear at all.

Imposter syndrome

Another paradox is that you need to look confident – that's why we follow you – but at the same time you have to live with all this uncertainty. Let's think about what this means. Your ambition got you the job, but now that you've arrived, it's all a lot more difficult than it looked from the outside. And you are still just you, but having to handle a whole lot more complexity than you have before. As you reach inside yourself to find the resources, it's not surprising that you feel more vulnerable than you ever have in the past. You feel like an imposter,[22] playing in the leader's role.

Blair Sheppard is the Dean of Duke University's Fuqua School of Business. He is also the former CEO and current Chairman of Duke Corporate Education. Blair is an innovator and a constant source of surprise. He always has a smile on his face and takes time for a conversation with everyone, from the janitor to the CEO. He cares genuinely for people and they love to follow him because he takes time to ask each individual how they are doing and to try and make their job a little better through each conversation.

Blair's reflection on leadership is 'you drove like crazy to get here and then you feel like the emperor with no clothes'. Because it's still just you, only now you are wearing the leader's suit. If you've seen the 2010 film *The Special Relationship*, which dramatises former UK Prime Minister Tony Blair's term in office from 1997 to 2007, you may recall the advice that former US President Bill Clinton is supposed to have given to Blair. He effectively told Blair that he should expect to feel completely overwhelmed by achieving the position of Prime Minister. However many years he has spent in preparation will not actually help him once he arrives. All the briefing and advice will have been about how to land the job – not about how to execute the job.

It's just the same for the leader. Getting the job and doing the job are two different things. It's common to feel uncertain once you are in place.

There is no 'right' answer

Leaders feel vulnerable. So if, inside, you sometimes find yourself thinking 'it's only me, I'll be found out soon enough' – don't worry, you are in good company. Remember what Ronnie Leten, the CEO of Atlas Copco, told us in Chapter 2? 'If the business isn't going well, you question yourself – is it me, or us?'

You need to accept that you will make the wrong decision from time to time and that you need to look confident despite this. In reality, in the complexity of today's global jungle, there is no one right way. There is a multiplicity of routes you could choose. The important thing is that whatever route you choose, when you set off, as you look over your shoulder, you see that people are actually following you. Many a 'right' decision has failed because no-one wanted to follow the leader.

> it's your job to be a convincing leader, whatever you feel like inside

It's not your job to be right all the time. It's your job to be a convincing leader, whatever you feel like inside.

By the way, if you are trying to manage upwards[23] with your CEO, it's a good idea to remember how vulnerable he or she might really be feeling. Be kind – and supportive. Understand that they don't have all the answers. When we put the leader on a pedestal, we aren't helping them to be as effective as we need them to be.

What if you don't think like this?

On a personal level, if you feel the tension and can't contain it, you will lose the loyalty of followers. Either they will try to avoid you, because of the tension you create, or they will lack confidence in your ability to steward them.

But there are bigger governance issues. If the Board to which the CEO reports is not *comfortable in discomfort* then there is the possibility for a dispute. If the Board needs facts, data and all the analysis before it will approve any decision, then its members are unlikely to approve a decision taken by the CEO based on this way of thinking. They will be looking for data and the CEO will tell them that there is insufficient. The CEO may push for a decision now, because to delay would mean falling behind, but they will want to wait until more facts are available. They will think that the CEO is ill-prepared. The CEO will think that they are moving too slowly and the enterprise may miss the moment of opportunity.

I wonder how many CEOs have lost their job through a dispute like this? (Or maybe it was the chair of the Board who lost out.) It would be interesting to re-visit some boardroom battles with this lens.

A final thought

Let's give the last word to an executive. A global world means that negotiations or important deals often take place by video or phone conference during the night. One leader, on one such call at 3 a.m., told the other side that, unless they hung up and called back at 3.45 a.m. with an agreed way forward, he was going to court to put the company into liquidation at 7 a.m. After much consternation and bluster ('that's a bit strong, isn't it?'), they called back at 3.45 a.m., in agreement. This leader's comment was: 'I can't remember the last time I wasn't "discomfortable".'

Developing *comfortable in discomfort* thinking: self assessment

As you reflect back on the ideas in this chapter, consider the following questions honestly for yourself:

▌ Can you live with grey, rather than the immediate certainty of a black and white answer? Can you call it even when the data isn't there?

▌ Can you learn to love ambiguity? Can you move forward effectively in ambiguity and not become frozen by uncertainty or driven to repeat earlier routines?

▌ Can you resist the temptation to close down the debate and decide? Can you hold back and stop yourself from driving to a conclusion? Can you create and hold the tension to reach a better answer?

▌ Can you retain the power of surprise? Can you hold your mind open to new ideas and change direction in a way that creates more value?

▌ Can you hold up and speak to an exciting future vision, even if the way forward isn't crystal clear? Can you hold your own vulnerability in check so that others have the courage to follow you?

As a leader, there will never be enough clarity, you often won't know the exact right next step for the enterprise, your decisions may be flawed and you will make mistakes. Yet, if you can think in this way, you will be able to make a good decision in the moment, without all the data. Or you will be able to delay taking a decision, even with all the information available to you, to get the timing right.

You won't be driven by the data. You will be in the driving seat.

Solid core

This chapter is in the centre of the book because it is at the heart of leadership.

Look at yourself. As a senior executive, you look the part of the leader. You seem confident and you can inspire confidence in others. You have learnt, painfully at times, to manage your outward appearance so that you can be a better leader. You have listened to the feedback and taken steps to change. Some things you changed so long ago that they now feel like natural parts of you.

Other changes are newer and you are still practising, sometimes getting it right, at other times getting it wrong. You know how important transparency and integrity are to observers – shareholders and stakeholders – in the twenty-first century and you do your best to live up to these heightened expectations.

What comes next?

Soul.

It doesn't sound very 'business-like', does it? More James Brown than Jack Welch. Yet, in my conversations with leaders throughout the world it was surprising how often that noun was used. I probed further to find out what the leaders I talked to really meant by soul. This chapter is about what I found and my interpretation of what leaders mean by soul.

Instinct

The truth is that, as a leader, you don't always know where you are going. Being strategic and visionary isn't at all easy in today's complex and networked world. But you do know where you are coming from. You have an instinct around the right thing to do. You have character and you lead from the inside out. You have what I call a *solid core.*

What does *solid core* mean? It means that even if you don't know where you are going, you need to understand where you are coming from. That is, you have to look inside and understand what is really important to you, the standards by which you live your life. You have to believe in yourself. You have to be grounded in something bigger than yourself. You have to have character. Your confidence has to be more than just skin deep.

> you need an inner compass that can keep you on the right path

The best metaphor for this way of thinking is a compass – an inner guidance mechanism. You need an inner compass that can keep you on the right path, even when others doubt your destination and means of getting there.

Put another way, it's about doing the right thing, having the conviction to do something which you believe leads to the correct route forward.

Conviction leadership

Sometimes the best stories of 'conviction leadership' come from the past. One is the story of Port Sunlight which was built by William Hesketh Lever (later Lord Leverhulme) on 56 acres near the River Mersey in England. The project was started in 1888 and represented the Quaker principles of capitalism. (If you look back, it's interesting to see how many modern organisations were founded on Quaker principles, from Amnesty International to Sony.) Quakers were trusted to be honest and founded many banks, including Barclays.

Port Sunlight was a beautiful garden village of houses built as homes for factory workers at the Lever Brothers soap factory (now part of Unilever). Sunlight was the name of their most popular cleaning agent. There was no expense spared. Lever enjoyed helping to plan the development and he employed nearly 30 different architects – each house was unique. The development also included allotments, a cottage hospital, schools, a concert hall, an open air swimming pool, a church and a temperance hotel. There was also the Lady Lever Art Gallery, where he displayed art that he collected from all over the world.[24]

Why did Lever do all this?

He wanted to socialise and Christianise business relations. He looked on it as profit sharing, but rather than share profits directly, he invested them in the village. He is quoted as saying: 'It would not do you much good if you send it down your throats in the form of bottles of whisky, bags of sweets, or fat geese at Christmas. On the other hand, if you leave the money with me, I shall use it to provide for you everything that makes life pleasant – nice houses, comfortable homes, and healthy recreation.'[25]

This is not to suggest that we should go back to this model today. What looked like enlightened capitalism at the tail end of Queen Victoria's reign (when, with no welfare system, people were dependent on the good-heartedness of employers not to exploit them) would now seem like paternalism.

Lever had strong values and they guided his business decisions to do the right thing by employees. He shared profits in the business with them – not a legal requirement – but the right thing to do. You will see in this chapter that this sentiment is still alive with leaders today, played out in modern ways.

The power of the modern enterprise

If you think about the power of a global company, organisations
like Google, it's daunting, compared with even 100 years ago.[26]
Of the 100 largest economies in the world, 51 are corporations;
only 49 are countries. The top 200 corporations' combined sales
are bigger than the combined economies of all countries minus
the biggest 10. While the sales of the top 200 are equivalent to
27.5 per cent of world economic activity, they employ only 0.78
per cent of the world's workforce.

What does this slew of statistics mean? It means that these
companies wield more power than national governments and
can move resources around the world in ways that sovereign
governments cannot. As a leader in one of these companies, you
have more power than a President or a Prime Minister. This is a
daunting and hugely challenging prospect.

> as a leader in one of these companies, you have
> more power than a President or a Prime Minister

Leaders need character

If the leaders of our giant corporations lack character; if they see
only short-term profit as their goal; if they cannot distinguish
straightforwardly between right and wrong, then we are
lost. Where regulation struggles to cross national or regional
boundaries, there is a moral imperative for self regulation. The
power of the too-powerful global company is an uneasy burden.
Like any leader, the corporation can choose to use its power for
good or for evil – and it is the leader who decides.

There is a wonderful scene in the film *Challenger* when the
actor playing Roger Boisjoly is trying to persuade his colleagues
that, despite inadequate data on which to take a fact-based
decision, it would be 'away from goodness' to launch.[27] This is
solid core thinking. He didn't have enough facts, but he had a

strong instinct that it would be too dangerous and he wanted to do the right thing – not move 'away from goodness'.

It's important to have a solid core, because as a leader you have this extraordinary power. It's important to use that power for good. As Google puts it, 'Don't Be Evil' – Google employees evoke this in meetings, to make sure that they take the right decisions.

Where does it come from?

Jasmine Whitbread of Save the Children expresses it well: 'I will admit to being grounded and confident. It's to do with my upbringing, I was supported by my parents and it counts.'

Niall FitzGerald, the Deputy Chairman of Thomson Reuters and former Chairman and CEO of Unilever (from 1996 to 2004) is even clearer. 'There are four characteristics of a leader: physical, emotional, intellectual and spiritual. Solid Core is about your soul: values, authenticity and integrity. You have to fall back on this regularly, because no facts will guide you at certain points in time.' Facts, the guiding light of MBA programmes worldwide, are not enough. If they were, leadership could be learnt by rote.

Another leader had a snappy definition for *solid core*: 'It's how you know where you need to be – a strong value system.'

What these statements all share is an inside-out view of leadership. The sentiment is one of sensing, or knowing, what to do; of being grounded and consistent inside. This is not something that can easily be measured.

Beyond executive thinking

There are several aspects to this way of thinking. The first is to find, test and learn to trust your own inner compass – your instinct around the right thing to do. Then, make sure everyone knows what you stand for, the personal standards that underpin how you work. The more people you lead, the less likely it is that you will spend time with each of them. You can't tell them what to do, but you can offer them a sense of the values to live by. Third, for every big decision, spend time thinking about the right thing to do – whatever the data may or may not be telling you.

Next, be authentic as a leader, but learn to balance the strong ego that got you the job with the capacity to be humble. In this complex world, no one person can know everything and you need to retain the capacity for humility and for learning from others.

First, let's consider what the phrase 'inner compass' means.

Inner compass

As we saw in Chapter 3, despite the emphasis in leadership books on 'vision', many executives may not know exactly where they are going, or how they are going to get there. What they do know is where they are 'coming from'. So the first point, as we unpick the meaning of *solid core*, is that leaders have a strong internal compass to guide them.

As a senior leader working in high levels of ambiguity and complexity, with such heightened visibility, it is fundamental that you know what you stand for, what you value; that you are grounded and secure in yourself. At the top, it is not enough to have a compelling picture of the future. You need internal resources to guide you when you are unsure how to frame the issue, or what the answer is.

> it is fundamental that you know what you stand for

One CEO expressed it clearly. 'I always go back to my instincts; you have to believe in yourself. It sounds introspective. You trust your own internal compass and combine this with external inputs – then I back my judgement. This is a massive intangible; inner confidence, but it has been proven over time. Obviously, you can't be wrong 9 times out of 10, so it also comes from your experience.'

What we are hearing is one CEO's version of his inner compass. For him, it is a combination of instinct, self-belief, experience and being proved right more often than wrong over the years. He doesn't talk of personal values. Recall that the simplicity of focusing on the way a leader thinks is that the underpinning belief system and the behaviours we observe can be as individual as the leader.

It's a way of thinking – not of doing or being.

Inner conviction

You remember from Chapter 2 Sim Tshabalala's struggle with being accused of being anti-Transformation, when he spoke out against some of the metrics being imposed on companies? 'I don't feel I have to act out my integrity, take me as I am, I will say what needs to be said. The Standard Bank Group has been colossally successful for 148 years, but it has an Anglo-Saxon world view, mechanistic, machine-like, a scientific cult of numbers. But I have always felt it's humane, like a body with parts we don't understand, but if you remove parts the body will die. A bunch of it is about the soul, humanity; less Aristotle, more Euripides.'

This is the kind of quote that sends you scurrying to Wikipedia, so here's the short version to save you the trip. Aristotle was the father of modern science, the first person to classify areas of human knowledge into distinct disciplines such as mathematics, biology and ethics. Some of these classifications are still used today. He is the father of logic and reasoning. Euripides, in contrast, was a poet and prolific playwright who went against the trend of the day in the fourth century BC by portraying slaves as intelligent and women as strong. He focused on the inner lives and motives of his characters, which was new to Greek audiences of the day.

So Sim is reflecting that you look inside yourself to find the way forwards; that it's about the soul, personal conviction.

Integrity

Niall FitzGerald is a great storyteller, with an ear for anecdote that is as sharp as his eye for ties (he has a colourful collection). Like so many leaders featured in this book, he is an upbeat, happy optimist. He explains his values by telling stories about his mother. 'Many of the corporate blunders of the last 10 years have been because leaders have asked "Is it legal?" rather than "Is it right?" We need to be soul searching about this. My mother told me: "If you take a decision you're not sure about, look in the mirror. If you can't look yourself in the eyes, you'll know it was the wrong decision".' He literally uses this test for himself, to gauge whether he is doing the right thing, not just what gets past the lawyers.

Stephen Green, the former Chairman of the HSBC Group, has even written a book about it.[28] It is possible to speculate that his values come from his religious convictions (he is an ordained Anglican minister, having studied at the Ming Hua Theological College while he was working in Hong Kong).

Stephen is a thoughtful and intellectual man, somewhat of an ascetic (despite the banking bonuses he receives, he is rumoured to give a lot of money to charity). He is well known for having spoken out against some of the excesses in his own industry, even before it became fashionable to do so. It is a testament to his objectivity that it was announced in September 2010 that he had been invited to join Vince Cable as Minister for Trade and Investment at the Department for Business, Innovation & Skills (BIS). (Vince Cable argues for breaking up the banks, who have become 'too big to fail'; Stephen against.)

Vince Cable welcomed his appointment and talked about Stephen's 'powerful philosophy for ethical business'.[29] In some ways it is back to the future – he started his career at the Ministry for Overseas Development before joining HSBC in 1982.

Stephen's book reflects his intellect and broad range of interests. His subject matter is the culture and morality of the global marketplace, which is under attack after the bank and corporate failures of the last two years. He argues for ethical and social integrity in the 'global bazaar', and to save market capitalism, the 'most powerful engine for development and liberation', from its dark side of also being 'a dangerous moral pollutant'.

Individual capacity for good

Stephen Green is not a naive person – he acknowledges the pitfalls and dangers of capitalism, as well as understanding the upside. His is the well-informed point of view that you would expect from a global executive, operating at the very highest level. Yet in some ways, his argument is also about the individual's capacity for taking the moral high road, so that capitalism can help us to a more sustainable future. He looks at human ambiguity and imperfection through his 'Christian prism'. It's a treatise to be good. And he is.

We started by talking about our inner compass. Now we have heard different CEOs agree with the idea, but then explore and explain it in different ways. Maybe it's experience, or standards, or values or soul – or simply integrity – who knows? Maybe it's some combination. What we do know for sure is that it's there. It's a strong internal guide to action.

Leaders barely reflect

Leaders are known for making change happen and for always being on the move. That's why we hire leaders. They are constantly dissatisfied with the status quo and always looking for improvement, new ways of doing business or expanding. If there is an intact system that just needs tending, we hire administrators. There's a big difference.

Precisely because of this, leaders are not so well known for being introspective or reflective. Reflection takes time and it means pausing in the relentless drive for change. However, the best leaders also make time for reflection – and have thought about the importance of the inner resources that underpin the individual.

Have you taken the time to reflect on what drives you? On what it means to do the right thing? Do you look in your own mirror as Niall FitzGerald recommends?

Let them share your compass

It's not enough just to have strong values and standards, even though they will guide your decision-making. They need to be clear to others too.

As CEO, you lead people you may never meet (if the company employs 300,000 or more people spread across the globe, how many can the CEO realistically meet?). Management is about helping others to get work done, advising and guiding their decisions and actions. Leadership is a lot more about telling them how to be. As a manager you will spend time with your people, even if not as much or as often as you would like. As a leader, they need to 'know' you without having met you. They need to know what you stand for, because that will guide their actions as surely as direct advice from their manager.

Niall FitzGerald puts it this way: 'As a leader, you speak into the biggest amplifier you have ever spoken into and the organisation will seek to respond; so be careful what you whisper and how you behave.'

When he was still CEO of Unilever, the consumer goods giant, he established a Code of Business Principles. Niall didn't want to call it a Code of Ethics, because a global business encompasses many different ethnicities and religions – so whose ethics would be the guide? But he did want a standard for doing business at Unilever where there were no shades of grey (or cultural relativism). The Code he established was absolute; if you breached it, you were fired. Niall said: 'Our brands belong to the consumers and we have to guard the reputation of our business on their behalf.' Niall enshrined the business values into a Code, so that they became a clear guide for everyone in the business, with no mitigating circumstances or escape clauses. He shared his values through a Code.

One of the leaders I admire most is Sir John Bond (appointed Chairman of Vodafone in July 2006). Although I haven't worked with him for about five years, whenever I worked with HSBC executives, until he left in 2006, I would ask them for stories about him. More than half the time, they had never had a conversation with the man. Yet the stories came thick, fast and consistent. 'When he leaves the office last, he always turns off the lights.' 'He doesn't always take a car if it's a short distance, he'll use public transport.' To this day, I have no idea if the stories were true or apocryphal. It doesn't matter. They thought they knew him and they were sure that he stood for careful husbandry of resources, for a cost-conscious approach to work – so they had this broad guidance to follow in their daily work.

I found the consistency, from Kuala Lumpur to Kingston, absolutely striking. Sir John was very clear about his values, his inner compass. And although he had not met every employee who told me a story about him, they were clear about his values too. They shared his compass through these stories.

Make it obvious

Jasmine Whitbread offers us a good story. Just after she joined Save the Children she started to pay attention to how there was no set of agreed values to guide the organisation – surprising when you understand their mission, that all children deserve a fair chance in life. And we tend to think of charities as values/conviction-driven organisations. They rely a lot on volunteers, who are mobilised by sharing similar values to the charity.

'We went through an interesting process – we asked about organisational values. There were eight and they were kept in a filing cabinet. One had a "but" in it! And people couldn't remember them. We went out to the whole organisation and had a conversation across it. We started with 50 countries and languages with a blank sheet of paper – we reminded them of our history and our mission.' (In Chapter 5, we will come to the importance of the past in shaping the future. In truth, Jasmine's sheet of paper was not entirely blank. They had history to guide them.)

'In the middle it was scary as a chief executive; pictures, metaphors, words, there was a riot of every value you can imagine. My thought was: "What if it comes back and it's not my values!" That I felt very strongly about. But it did come back with my values – not just mine, but the organisation's values as well. We didn't have to roll them out, they were already here.'

As a person with strong values, Jasmine came in to lead an organisation founded on strong conviction – as many charities are. She joined because she identified strongly with its aims and beliefs. (We will see in Chapter 6 that the CEO has to align their personal values with the organisation. There might be give and take on both sides – the CEO might adopt a new value, or might add one to the organisation – but basically, there has to be a fit.)

But beyond the question of fit, there is the imperative for others to understand how your values, or your personal foundation for your inner compass, feature in your life. Not just that you have a compass, but what it is and how it guides you. And let them share it.

New into her role at Save the Children, Jasmine started that process at scale. It was an ambitious project across 50 (at that stage, relatively independent) countries. As a result, Save the Children now has a well articulated set of values. And, at the same time, they have also learnt what Jasmine stands for.

The right thing to do

The underlying refrain from so many of these conversations, whether it was about moving to a global structure, or changing the business model, or any other big decision that would change the shape or direction of the enterprise, was often 'because it's the right thing to do'. How can you decide the 'right thing', when often, as we saw in Chapter 3, you don't have sufficient information?

As Niall FitzGerald said: 'Observers of leadership underestimate the instinctive nature of it. We hone and polish our instincts.' And they all have instinct, these CEOs. An irrational guide to rational decisions.[30]

Which leaders do we really admire?

Despite the power that these CEOs of global companies wield, they don't tend to be the exemplars that business people cite. For years, when I've asked executives to identify a leader they admire, they have most often named a leader of society, or a general, or even a politician, but rarely a business leader. Try it for yourself. One executive even said 'there are very few corporate leaders that inspire me'. Mandela and Gandhi are the two names most often chosen. Their stories are well known, so we won't dwell on them for long. And then let's think about what they tell us.

Nelson Mandela led South Africa into a peaceful post-apartheid era; in 1993 he won the Nobel Peace Prize with F.W. de Klerk, for dismantling apartheid. This man was jailed for 28 years under intense duress. On Robben Island, prisoners were locked up 23 hours a day and conditions could be extremely cold. Yet when Dennis Healey, the British politician, visited him in 1970, 20 years before his release, he didn't complain, but spent the two-hour visit finding out as much as he could about world affairs and the European attitude towards apartheid. Dennis Healey said: 'It was very unusual for white people to respect black people, but he exerted great moral authority. I would say he's a saintly person: he was never vindictive against the people who demonized him. When you think what he went through for all those years in jail, it's amazing how intact he is mentally as well as morally. He's a good man with a capital G.'[31] Bill Clinton said something similar: 'Every time Nelson Mandela walks into a room we all feel a little bigger, we all want to stand up, we all want to cheer, because we'd like to be him on our best day.'[32]

Mandela's story is one of endurance, of undying belief and conviction that one day apartheid would end and blacks and whites would live together on equal terms. He is not a religious man as far as we know – but his ability to keep his eye on a long-term goal, despite insane hardship and obstacles, speaks to an inner conviction that sustains him.

Gandhi's story is similar. Like Mandela, he trained as a lawyer. He was a political activist all his life, starting in 1906 protesting against fingerprinting Indians in South Africa, and culminating with the Quit India movement against the British Raj in the 1940s. Unlike Mandela, he maintained a strict policy of nonviolence and would use marches and hunger strikes in peaceful protest. He, too, was frequently jailed for his actions.

Is this too daunting?

Both men had a strong sense of what was right and what was wrong. Each was prepared for extraordinary sacrifice and long-term commitment to overcome injustice. They wanted to do the right thing, whatever the cost to them personally. And they are cited as the best leaders, the most admired, because of this.

Does this sound daunting? As a business leader, can you be admired and lauded like these legendary men? Their stories and their commitment to justice may have elevated this idea to the level where you don't think you could possibly keep up. That's not the point. What this classroom exercise demonstrates is that executives aspire to be 'good'. They would like to be known for overcoming adversity and doing the right thing, despite tremendous odds. On one occasion a (male) executive chose Mother Theresa as his aspirational leader. His comment was: 'If you had interviewed her, she would have had all five of these ways of thinking – and she kept developing too.'

We know that leaders think in the same way, even if the scope and scale of their decisions and actions may not have the same impact as these heroes, and even if their tenure is not as long and their decisions have less impact on society as a whole. They have the same instinct.

That's why Stephen Green of HSBC was invited into the government – because he can be trusted to do the right thing, arguing against accepted ways of doing business in the banking industry. In 2009, he was quoted observing: 'Underlying all these events is a question about the culture and ethics of the industry. It is as if, too often, people had given up asking whether something was the right thing to do, and focused only on whether it was legal and complied with the rules. The industry needs to recover a sense of what is right and suitable as a key impulse for doing business.'[33]

Rise above the politics

One CEO told me: 'I am passionate about doing the right thing for our business. I tell people to understand the politics but don't get in the middle of it; avoid the political quagmire.'

Every organisation has politics – the bigger the organisation, the messier they are and the more difficult to understand. The problem with organisational politics is that they can steer you off course and you can end up doing whatever it takes to save your reputation, or to avoid getting fired.

Some of the worst politics are created when an organisation has a culture of fear. This sounds like something you'd say about Dickensian England, or Russia during the Cold War.[34] It sounds odd to say it about a modern corporation in the twenty-first century, but it is true.

> some of the worst politics are created when an organisation has a culture of fear

It can be driven by the purest of motives, for example, a desire to be the best in the business and to get everything absolutely right. Soon, being the best means that failure is not an option. After this, risk-taking dies. Then, you find yourself sending emails to justify your actions or cover your tracks. You are so busy not making a mistake, or justifying your actions, that you lose sight of what you could achieve. The game is defensive, not offensive. And doing the right thing is about playing to win, not about playing to avoid losing.

Don't underestimate what it takes to do the right thing in a culture of fear. You can go from hero to zero pretty fast.

Modern conviction?

The story of Lord Leverhulme and Port Sunlight was an
example of conviction leadership in the nineteenth century.
In the aftermath of the 2008 financial services' crisis, with
the nature and role of banks and business being debated, the
conversation today revolves around 'responsible capitalism'.
(Irresponsible capitalism still centres around issues like
exploiting child labour, a world that Lord Leverhulme would
recognise.) Capitalism as it has played out in a largely post-
communist world is increasingly seen as an unsatisfactory
proposition. The notion of making capitalism responsible again
includes a range of ideas. For some, it is about adding social
responsibility and charitable activities to the corporate agenda;
for others, it is worrying about how to influence the short-term
outlook of some shareholders, who seem more interested in
personal or institutional wealth than the long-term survival of
the companies in which they invest.

The right thing to do can get big and messy when you are a
leader in a global organisation. When you decide to stand up and
be counted, the audience is large and critical. And the challenges
facing modern business are partly about redefining the right
thing to do for us all, not just for the individual business.

Authenticity

Leadership books place a lot of emphasis on authenticity. The
definition of authenticity refers to the truthfulness of origins,
attributions, commitments, sincerity, devotion and intentions.
Authenticity is about the human need to be led by someone
who can be trusted, who is honest and sincere.

There are a couple of reasons for this. Obviously, no-one likes
being lied to. If someone lies to you, you are being manipulated
– you don't have all the information you need and they are in
control, not you. Anderson carried out research into the values

we most and least admire. 'Honest' was ranked top of his long (555) list of values and liar was bottom.[35]

We have deeply rooted notions of fairness and we know that every system has free riders (people who coast on the back of work that others do) and so we watch out for them. But it turns out that we are not all good at spotting liars. Researchers videotaped a group of second-year MBA students as they pretended to interview for a job. (It's interesting just how much research into executive behaviour is actually based on studying business school students.) Half the interviewees were entirely truthful, while half told at least three lies that they thought would make them more attractive candidates for the (fake) job.

The scientists then showed these videos to a second set of people and asked them to rate the honesty of the interviewees and say which ones they'd hire. The results – people who said they think that most people are basically honest, good-natured, and kind were better at spotting the liars than the self-described cynics. Subjects who were more suspicious were, ironically, less likely to detect, and more likely to hire, the liars.[36] It's the opposite of 'it takes one to know one'!

We are supposed to follow leaders and there is an unwritten rule that we should be able to trust where they are taking us. So there is a premium on being authentic.

Being yourself is not enough

So leaders worry a lot about authenticity and rightly so. But it's important not to confuse authenticity with acting exactly as you would with close friends or family.

As soon as you step into the leadership role, expectations of you change. Inside, you know it's still just you. One of my favourite questions to senior executives is 'how old do you feel inside?' Most confess to somewhere between 13 and 18 (and this question is often posed and answered in public!).

Now imagine a world in which these leaders acted out the age they feel. Teenagers are self-obsessed – with their looks, with their clothes and with their gadgets. They spend hours preening. They lack confidence, because they are still trying to understand who they are. They move in packs (because when you are still unsure who you are, you gain confidence from being the same as your peers). They profess individuality and difference, but just want to fit in. They communicate with each other, but not with those outside their peer group, especially not with adults. Boys particularly seem to lose the ability to speak. (When my godson was in his teens, I used to insist on a full sentence from him at least once a visit – it caused almost physical anguish.) How long would you follow with confidence a leader who acted like this? It's almost a perfect description of the anti-leader.

How old do you feel inside? Do you act your age – or as the leader they need you to be?

The art of leadership is being close and distant at the same time. Close enough to understand what followers need, distant enough to lead them. Close enough to understand what's going on, on the ground, distant enough to manage it. Close enough to hear the new ideas, distant enough to choose objectively between them.

> the act of leadership is incredibly conscious, even self conscious

So the act of leadership is incredibly conscious, even self conscious. We'll come back to this idea in Chapter 6. Authenticity then is not as easy as 'being yourself'. It takes some reflection and it takes some work. It's about reaching inside yourself to become the leader that your followers need.

Humility (keep it real)

There is no 'I' in leader. It is a motivational-poster cliché, but that does not make it any less true.

As Jasmine Whitbread says, 'I'm far from perfect. Humility is important.' No 'I' here means that, somehow, you have to retain or develop a sense of humility. Why 'somehow'? Because a CEO gets the job for a variety of reasons; talent, luck and drive are among them. There are two other pieces to this puzzle. The first is an overweening desire for the job. Whether you see this as a heightened sense of responsibility, a desire for ever-increasing levels of accountability or outrageous ambition, the end result is the same. Leaders really, really want the job.

Leaders also have a well developed ego. It's an important part of the package. It's what keeps them on track, maintains their self-confidence and enables them to bounce back after a setback.

Being a member of a senior team is quite different from all the advice you received as a junior manager about teambuilding – being a good team member, building a balanced team. By definition, the most senior team is made up of the most ambitious, most dedicated and most confident individuals, all of whom have carved a highly successful career path. They don't necessarily balance each other well and co-working is built on alliances, negotiation and respect. There is no doubt that some level of co-operation between the team members is vital to the prosperity of the organisation, and their support for the CEO is critical. In fact, some will be there because they are loyal beyond question to the CEO, and any foibles and inadequacies will be tolerated.

Retain a well developed ego

If you try to enter the hothouse atmosphere of the executive team on the basis of the standard advice on teambuilding and getting along with others, you will fail. You should have a robust ego and hold on to it, alongside the other egos in the room. So humility isn't always natural for a leader.

Followers have a tendency to tell you what a great leader you are. And there is a chronic lack of feedback at the CEO level. Everyone wants to impress the boss. It's a bit like working in Hollywood. The studio knows that a good actor makes them money and so they invest a lot in building their esteem. Leaders tend to get similar treatment – it's almost as if you become superhuman. So the ego is strong and that's a good thing.

But at the same time, you have to manage to keep yourself realistic about your own capabilities. How do you remember that, while you have to make the ultimate call, other people also did a lot of work to get you to the decision point? How do you keep listening? As Jim Collins puts it, how do you look into the mirror to accept accountability and out of the window to acknowledge achievement?[37]

Hold on to vulnerability

Leaders are vulnerable. We talked about this in Chapter 3. An anonymous quote demonstrates this really clearly. 'The CEO is a narcissistic and insecure man and I upset him. I thought about this feedback and my options; whether or not to change behaviour and if so, what and how. You have to be able to listen when people are willing to touch you on the shoulder, give you feedback and stop you getting to the end of the rope and falling off the platform. I decided to charm the pants off the CEO. I put right a relationship that shouldn't have gone wrong. I over-communicate, over-care and in every circumstance I make sure he is OK. For example, he's shy, so at parties, I stay by his side and take care of him.'

There is a tendency to think that the boss has it all under control and that you are the only one who is struggling with uncertainty. It's not true. The boss is vulnerable too. And as long as we don't let the vulnerability disable us, then it keeps us humble, listening and open to others' ideas.

As a leader, there must be a big temptation to surround yourself with 'yes' people. You need to do the opposite: don't hide away. As one CEO advised, 'At work, don't become insular, talk to clients and competitors, listen to your own radical thinkers.'

Don't hide away

It was a crowded and awkwardly shaped room for networking. There were too many tables, chairs and serving points for the dinner that was about to arrive to allow for easy movement around the room. People were nervous – this was their opportunity to network with the great and the good in the company. Networking at this level can be a double-edged sword – you get exposure – and it could all go wrong. There was a sudden swell of chatter and laughter – the executives were here. They could be seen walking across the square towards the tiny restaurant and then entering one by one through the restaurant door. They spread themselves around the room, intent on making the group feel at ease and on meeting as many people as possible.

There was one exception. The leader of this executive team started well. He had an intense approach to the task in hand and fixed upon each person in turn, asking serious, business-related questions. There was no social chit chat with this man. At the same time he had a winning smile that he deployed to great effect, to alleviate some of the intensity. People were slightly 'at attention' as they responded to the acute scrutiny – definitely on their mettle.

When it came to time for dinner, the executives were spread around the tables, to continue in conversation. As if at some hidden signal, three guests who had arrived with the executive committee headed for the same table as the most senior executive and sat around him. He relaxed visibly. They were attentive, smiling and laughing a lot. His attention to others waned. What happened? Did he have serious business to address with these three? Was he introverted and so had used all his available energy in the networking before dinner? Who knows. This wasn't a one-off – he was a repeat offender. As his more junior colleagues continued to socialise, he switched off and relaxed. He was hiding in full sight.

Get good feedback

Like it or not, the leader is surrounded by sycophants – it's the hardest position from which to hear it like it is, because people want to pass good news to you. And let's face it, you are very talented. A lot of the accolades are deserved.

But as a leader, you can become remote from reality. The power that goes along with the position, the executive perks such as the executive jet, the personal assistant, the lavish expense account and the chauffeured limousine, can make you lose perspective. When you start to believe yourself above the common laws that bind others, then you are in trouble as an executive. It takes strength of character not to believe your own press.

> it takes strength of character not to believe your own press

Martin Spurling of HSBC deliberately follows a plan to keep himself in touch with his own limitations. 'People tell you what you want to hear. I think I'm quite good at people skills, but people stop giving you feedback when you get more senior and just tell you how good you are, if they say anything. Luckily I have a circle of close friends who I rely on to give me honest feedback, so there is no chance of me getting an inflated view of myself.'

Another CEO looks to his family and friends to stop him becoming too self-important. 'In your personal life, having a wife and family who don't think you rule the world at all. It's almost like there is something in the air conditioning in the car that blows on you – on the way to work it changes you into someone people listen to, on the way home it changes you into someone no-one listens to! Having support and friendship at home, not being idolised, bring a balance to your personality.'

Both of these successful CEOs have found a safe way of getting outside opinion. Do you always need external stimulus to keep you humble? Maybe not. Maybe you already have a natural sense of humility. If you do, keep and safeguard it. More than one CEO has lost the job, often humiliatingly and publicly, through hubris and arrogance.

What if you fail?

And if we think about it, isn't it easy to see when an executive isn't grounded? The opposite of a solid core isn't a rotten core. It's more that the leader may lack the internal conviction or confidence to have the instinct around the right thing to do. We talk about people who have 'a chip on their shoulder'. You know that they are preoccupied with proving something or denying something and it gets in the way.

You find leaders who can't delegate because they think they can do a better job; others who need to be seen as the best on the block and so use their intellect cruelly to belittle others; some who like to leap ahead to a decision without taking others with them to show how smart they are. In every case they have something to prove. As a leader, you have made it and you have nothing left to prove.

> as a leader, you have made it and you have nothing left to prove

Can you think of an example of someone like this in your own life? Try to think of someone you know who has a sound inner compass, and someone else who doesn't.

The enterprise will suffer

At the enterprise level, if you lose your instinct, the whole organisation will suffer. At that point, you have to be ready to accept accountability – after all, as you will find in the next chapter, it happened on your watch and you are ultimately accountable. You have to step up and take it on the chin, like BP's Tony Hayward, whose story is told in Chapter 6. You got the plaudits – now it's time to take the blame.

There have been some spectacular business failures over the past decade. Enron, Worldcom and Lehman Brothers were the largest bankruptcies in US history during this period. The Enron story[38] makes unhappy reading, with several of the most senior executives of the corporation indicted and sentenced to many years in jail. The former chief financial officer, Fastow, and his wife Lea both pleaded guilty to charges against them. Fastow was sentenced to ten years with no parole in a plea bargain to testify against Lay (former Chairman and then CEO), Skilling (former CEO) and Causey (former chief accounting officer). In May 2006, Skilling was convicted of 19 out of 28 counts of securities fraud and wire fraud and was sentenced to 24 years in prison.[39] Lay was convicted of all 6 counts of securities and wire fraud for which he had been tried. He faced a total of up to 45 years in prison, but he died in July 2006, before sentencing. Causey was sentenced to 7 years for disguising the company's financial shape during his tenure. In total, 16 people pleaded guilty for crimes committed at the company.

Clearly this is an exceptional story and the intent is not to imply that lacking a solid core means that you end up in jail. A leader without a solid core may falter or misstep just through getting mired in organisational politics or through lacking humility and overestimating personal capabilities.

However, recall the statistics given earlier in this chapter about the enormous power that is wielded by the leaders of the very largest global corporations. When it goes wrong, as it did at Enron, the consequences are enormous. When huge success turns to huge failure, the fallout is widespread and long-lasting. People lose their jobs, reputations are sullied and instead of adding value and creating more wealth, value is destroyed.

Leaders need to think *solid core* to keep them honest, to keep them in touch with reality and to help them to take the right decisions.

A final thought

Let's close the chapter as we started it. A solid core is at the heart of leadership. It means that underpinning your decisions and your actions, people can see a consistency in approach. They may not always know which decision you will take, or which path you will choose, but your reasoning has an identity and a quality that they recognise. They see that you are grounded in a way that gives them confidence. There is a sense of purpose about you.

The essence of a solid core is that you relax into having 'made it'. This gives you the confidence and inner certainty to become the leader your followers need, rather than still trying to prove that you deserve the job. When I am asked to coach people who lack this inner compass, I pass on the best piece of advice that was ever given to me. 'You've made it – you have nothing left to prove – now be generous with what you have learnt.'

You sense the right thing to do.

Where does this inner certainty come from? As we have seen, it's as diverse as the leaders themselves. For some, like Stephen Green, their values have a religious base. For others, like Jasmine Whitbread and Niall FitzGerald, it comes from a nurturing upbringing. It may come from a mixture of experience and a strongly supportive, but honest, family and circle of friends. There is likely to be not just one source, but a myriad of influences. The result is that you think with a personal inner compass that gives you a values-driven approach to business and to the world.

Developing *solid core* thinking: self assessment

Test your own *solid core*. Be candid in your answers to the following questions:

■ Do you have an inner compass? Do you live your life according to clear personal values? Do you have irreproachable integrity?

■ Do you share this inner compass with others? Do people know what these values are? Can they see how these standards guide your decisions and actions?

■ Do you have an internal sense of the right thing to do? Can you rise above the politics? Can you demonstrate your internal conviction in ways that others can see?

■ Are you authentic? Do you know that this is not just the same as being yourself?

■ Do you show humility? At the same time, can you retain a strong ego? Do you have the courage not to surround yourself with cronies? Can you keep open to others' real opinion of you?

chapter

5

On my watch

We have now reached the fourth way of thinking. The core idea in this chapter is that you only serve for a period of time. As a leader, you inherit the organisation from others and, as you step away, new people take over. Sounds obvious, doesn't it? But many leaders spend too much time on today, bound up in the mesmeric dance, as if they were contestants on the UK TV show *Strictly Come Dancing*, so focused on learning the next few steps that they can't remember if the dance is a waltz or a polka, or what the dance after next is planned to be.

The metaphor here is that it's like a sailor making an ocean crossing, or round the world voyage. You take your turn on watch, but it only lasts for a while, then someone else takes over. And one day you'd better be ready for your watch to end.

In the zone

The story of Lou Gerstner's turnaround of IBM is legendary. It's also an excellent example of a leader who is effective at managing in three time zones at the same time.

Gerstner joined IBM as Chairman and CEO in 1993 and was shocked to realise how bad the situation was. He immediately turned his attention to the most pressing issue – making the company solvent. Under his guidance, IBM cut billions in expenses (partly through massive layoffs) and raised cash by selling assets. Gerstner says that few people even understood how perilously close the company was to running out of cash.

He stopped a plan, which was already well under way, to break up the company into several operating units. Gerstner characterises this as 'the most important decision I ever made – not just at IBM, but in my entire business career'.[40] The rationale behind it was to leverage all of the pieces of IBM – hardware, services and software – to deliver top-to-bottom technology solutions.

Culture was holding them back

What Gerstner came more slowly to realise was that, more than anything else, the culture of the company was holding it back and heading it for disaster. 'Culture is everything', he observed. Executives spoke in 'code' and decisions lacked the rigorous, cost-driven analysis that he had been expecting.[41] Rather than work together as a team, divisions competed against each other both internally and in the field. Management 'presided rather than acted', and the entire company was dangerously preoccupied with itself rather than with customers.

He and his advisors decided to tie employee compensation to the performance of the whole company rather than to the employee's particular division. This, the thinking went, would force them to co-operate and venture outside of the fiefdoms in which they operated. Employees needed to know that their competitors were outside of IBM, not across the corridor.

He also wanted to rid the company of 'obsessive perfectionism' and 'studying things to death'. In the new IBM, people would be rewarded for getting things done fast. Gerstner says he estimated it would take five years to turn around IBM's culture. He underestimated. In some ways, it's still a work in progress (if you read the sections on DNA later in this chapter, you'll see why).

Lou Gerstner is a private man and quick to acknowledge others. He believed that employees also realised that IBM had to change or die. Speaking at Harvard in 2002, he told MBA students that he did not see himself as the white knight saviour of IBM. Instead, change was successful because of the pride and energy of the employees themselves. And in his book *Who Says Elephants Can't Dance?*, telling the story of the turnaround, he is careful to acknowledge the proud history of the company, which he harnessed to help save it.

What made Gerstner successful?

Lou Gerstner didn't walk away from IBM's history, even though the route to a successful future required a much more collaborative culture than its individualistic past. He acknowledged it and integrated it into the present, in order to build the future. This integration of three time zones – past, present and future – is critical.

But in that drive towards a place at the top, success is often about today, not yesterday or tomorrow. The pressure to perform in the short term is relentless and you face an unforgiving audience if you falter. And let's face it, the future will be in someone else's hands, it will be someone else's success – so why not focus on today? It may help you to get it into perspective if you acknowledge that it is only yours for a while.

> the future will be in someone else's hands

As the leader of an organisation, you inherit its past; you manage its present; and you plan for its future. So it's not so much about what you leave behind, but about how you manage these three time zones. That's what this way of thinking is about.

What will happen while you lead?

And you only have it for a limited period, from about three to ten years. It's what happens while you are leading that matters. Let's think about what it's like for you today.

You spend a lot of your time running the business of the day in your executive role. You probably feel a bit guilty about it and so, as you pass through airports to take yet another plane to a remote meeting, you sometimes pick up a business book. It might be about strategic agility, or visionary thinking – some topic to help you to spend more time thinking ahead and less on today's business and the next quarter's results.

You know that you should have a 5–10-year time horizon looking ahead to the future of the business. You think quite often about the legacy that you will leave behind when you retire, your gift to the organisation or to the industry. So your diary is mostly about the business of the day, with at least a nod ahead.

What is your next step?

It's to put into context the bit part that you are playing in a much longer movie. It's a story that was started before you arrived and will continue after you have left.

> you consciously allocate effort to be spent on the past, present and future

Can you live in three time zones, without getting jetlag? Can you think about your role being loaned to you, just for now? Think *on my watch*. With this way of thinking, you consciously allocate effort to be spent on the past, present and future, rather than spending too much effort only on business today. You understand why the past matters to your organisation and you know how to make it relevant today, as well as in the future. You spend sufficient time on keeping the enterprise prosperous today, but you also know how to delay gratification – to postpone the excitement of immediate success by laying the groundwork for future success. You can move effectively between the three time zones and don't get too caught up in any of them for too long.

You know that you have been lent the organisation for a limited amount of time and you reflect on this. What will happen on your watch?

Past, present and future

Jacko Maree, the Group CEO of Standard Bank, got it immediately. This is what he said. 'I like this. I love the idea that you have to be careful of your heritage, if you have been successful over a long time then it's worth saving. It is more than just the company's history, it is also the lessons of the past. I think I spend my time 15 per cent on the past, 50 per cent on the present and 35 per cent on the future. You better bloody well make sure the shop is working today (the analysts push here); budgets, people issues, government. Then you also need to spend enough time on what will grow the business in the future. I really like the description. Like ambiguity, it's the issues of today in the context of who you are as a company and then spend enough time thinking about growth for the future.'

Balancing act

What we are talking about here is balancing heritage, current returns and growth. As Jacko says, you can't spend all of your time in any one time zone, despite the vociferous clamour of the market analysts demanding attention to the next quarter's business results. With so much market pressure, this can become your default time zone – but it won't be the one that ensures your legacy.

When you think like this as a leader, it means that you respect the past and, as Jacko says, you learn from it as well. While some statistics on company life expectancy can be unsettling (look at the turnover in the FTSE 100 and the Fortune 500), there are still companies around today which have been in business for over one hundred years. Some are in the same business that they started, like Standard Bank, which has been in banking for nearly 150 years. They have some wonderful sepia photographs of their first banks, which were roadside tents.

Some have changed business dramatically, like Nokia. Many teenagers think Nokia is a Japanese company. In fact, this stylish Finnish mobile phone company started out in 1865 as a paper manufacturer, set up by mining engineer Fredrik Idestam on the banks of the Tammerkoski rapids in Tampere, southwestern Finland.[42] The point here is that both companies have a strong legacy to safeguard and to perpetuate.

The Nokia example shows that respecting the past isn't the same as keeping the past. A series of leaders have proved adept at keeping Nokia moving, changing and responding to market opportunities, so that they are as relevant today as they were 145 years ago – just in a completely different industry now. This is an important distinction – to be able to respect the past, but, at the same time, not to be restricted by it.

Remember to add the future to the mix

And the final piece of the puzzle is thinking about the future. This is where we get into the 'guilty' conversation. Textbooks have been advising leaders for years to be more forward-looking, to have a 5–10-year time horizon. Most will sheepishly confess to spending insufficient time thinking ahead, because they are just too busy keeping the show on the road.

I am pleasantly surprised by the positive response in the classroom to a simple exercise on time management. Executives are asked to draw three circles, labelled past, present and future, with the size of each circle representing the amount of time they spend in each time zone, and we discuss the results.

Mostly it helps to remind them to spend more time thinking broadly as well as forwards. It is a wide view of the world (thinking about issues not directly related to their business – political, social, economic, technological) that helps them to be more thoughtful about the range of future options. (There is a cultural aspect to this exercise, covered later in this chapter.)

> spend more time thinking broadly as well as forwards

We all like to laugh at the idea of the two-day strategy retreat, because it suggests that the leadership team only spends two days a year thinking about the future. If you do this exercise for yourself, honestly, and the 'future' circle that you draw is disproportionately small, you should be concerned. How can you develop the self-discipline to spend more time thinking ahead?

The real skill here is to keep all three time zones in your head simultaneously. There is a lot of advice out there telling you that, as a leader, you should 'live in the future'. That simply isn't true. The trick is to spend enough time in each of the three zones – simultaneously.

Why the past matters

Let's return to Standard Bank. Sim Tshabalala, Deputy Group CEO, has a unique perspective on why the past matters. 'I have enormous reverence for the company history and use that to identify our DNA. I love where the bank is coming from, inextricably woven into the fabric of society. We have always been outside South Africa (since the 1880s); we have always been big. We have been here nearly 150 years, what are we doing today that will have them talking about us in 150 years?'

Sim successfully bridges from the past to the future. He can see that the past (148 years) should provide a clear bridge to the next 150 years, through actions taken today. How many executives do you know with a 150-year future horizon? Not so many? And we hear again his refrain about nation-building. He sees the bank as part of the fabric of society, to sustain and build the environment. He doesn't see it as a separate entity, out to make as much money as possible for shareholders.

It's the DNA

And Sim uses these few sentences to raise another critical point. The bank's DNA is created through its history. As James Watson and Francis Crick's famous publication in 1953[43] tells us, DNA is the hereditary material in humans and almost all other organisms. Nearly every cell in a person's body has the same DNA and it can make copies of itself. When cells divide, each new cell has an exact copy of the DNA present in the old cell.

In organisational terms, each new hire quickly learns what works and what doesn't from existing employees. Human beings are social creatures and we like to fit in, so the 'rules', or DNA, are soon passed on. The past has extraordinary power over the present.

When you are 150 years old, DNA seems a much more appropriate way of describing the belief structure of the organisation. The modern description tends to talk about 'culture'[44] or 'the way we do things around here'. But the modern description makes leaders believe that culture is just another piece of organisational software that they can manipulate. When it's described as DNA, two things happen. The first is that you realise it's not so trivial or malleable – as Lou Gerstner found at IBM.

The second thing that happens is that you realise how important the past is to a sustainable future. It is not something to be discarded lightly.

Look out IBM

Fujitsu is big in Japan, but less known elsewhere. It's 75 years old and the third biggest player in the global IT services market, with sales of 4.6 trillion yen (US$50 billion) and 172,000 employees in 60 countries. It also has a distinguished track record as a technology pioneer. In 1954, Fujitsu developed the first Japanese computer and in 1976 it created the first Japanese supercomputer. Among many other firsts, Fujitsu engineers created the first computer with Japanese language capability in 1979.

Historically, IBM was the giant and Fujitsu the pesky upstart. Now, under the leadership of its new president, Masami Yamamoto, Fujitsu is set on change – intent on moving out of Big Blue's shadow. Yamamoto, the youngest president of the company for thirty years, brings a more modern style of leadership and a new perspective – he talks about going on the offensive.

Yamamoto visited more than 100 corporate customers within the first three months of being president. Research by Fujitsu's corporate brand office found that understanding of what the company did and stood for was often very limited in the global marketplace. So based on this research, they are launching a new brand promise: 'Shaping tomorrow with you'. And just like Jasmine in her search to uncover the values of Save the Children, Fujitsu finds that their future is embedded in their past.

The phrasing may be new, but people within the company agree that what it describes is quintessentially Fujitsu. 'The company's brand promise "Shaping tomorrow with you" is a new way of describing what we have always stood for,' says president Yamamoto. 'It is already in our DNA, but stating it in this way crystallises what makes us different. It is a catalyst for change.' DNA can be a powerful way of relating future change to past success – it makes the change more likely to stick.

Uncovering the depth of the DNA

Try this exercise in your own organisation. It's called the
Culture Wall (maybe it should be called the DNA Wall) and
the instructions are simple. Give each of your team members
a piece of flipchart paper to hang landscape style on the wall.
Ask each person to draw a timeline that highlights significant
events, which in that person's view have helped to shape
what you stand for as an organisation today. For example, a
significant expansion or acquisition; the day a key executive
joined or left; an innovation or experiment. The discussion is
even better if it is held with a mixture of some younger and
some more seasoned executives, so that generational knowledge
can be passed down in the time-honoured human way –
through storytelling.

> draw a timeline that highlights significant events

It is eye-opening to see how far back in time these stories on
the wall start. Often they will start with events that pre-date the
day that any of the executives in the room actually joined the
organisation. Sometimes they start with stories that were learnt
by the most long-serving executives from their predecessors.
At other times, one or more individuals will have researched
the past independently and will have stories about founders or
leaders they only know by reputation. It's then that you realise
the culture really runs deep.

The other interesting aspect to the conversation is how proud
the people are of the organisation's heritage. It's a bit like the
UK TV series *Who Do You Think You Are?*, where genealogists
research the background of celebrities. The celebrities at some
point always become emotional as they discover aspects of their
heredity that were previously unknown to them – their sense of
pride is palpable. Leaders underestimate the sense of pride and
belonging employees feel and how easily it can be evoked.

The nugget for you as a leader is not to fall into the common trap of thinking that culture can be changed easily or quickly. It's like trying to teach your grandpa to hip hop, when he has spent his entire life jiving. It takes new skills, uses different muscles and won't even begin to be successful if you start by rubbishing the jive as a dance.

Respect the past

This can happen to a leader in any walk of life. For those who like English football, you'll probably remember Brian Clough's short reign as manager of Leeds United from July to September 1994. Clough, the ex-player turned manager, was sacked by the Leeds directors after only 44 days. He had the least successful run with the team of any full-time manager, winning only one match in six games. Yet he wasn't an unsuccessful manager, in fact his achievement of winning back-to-back European Cups with Nottingham Forest is thought to be one of the finest records in football history. He is also considered to be one of the greatest English managers never to manage the England team. So what went wrong?

Clough was not known for his tact and had strong views. It was widely known that he did not respect the tactics of his predecessor, Don Revie, and wanted to make changes at Leeds. Clough was reported as saying, at an early training session with the team, 'you can throw all your medals in the bin, because they were not won fairly'.[45] Only those who were there at the time can know if this is true. Whether or not he used exactly those words, Clough had a reputation for being outspoken and impatient for change. Yet making changes by breaking with the past is a dangerous route. Do you have a deep understanding and respect for the history of the enterprise that you currently safeguard? Do you understand how the culture was built, how the purpose has played out over the years and why the organisation exists in its current form?

Don't just observe it, understand what to do with it

Sir John Tusa is clear that a leader needs to understand an organisation's past, in order to lead it successfully towards its future. 'It's a disaster if there is a gap between what the organisation and what the leader thinks. Look at John Birt and the BBC, Birt thought the BBC values were rubbish. It leads to ineffectiveness, if not worse.'

In his tenure as BBC Director General from 1992 to 2000, Birt was widely criticised for adopting the then Conservative government's market policies too enthusiastically. He created internal markets at the BBC that led to a lot of outsourcing (corporate speak for finding external suppliers), while internal BBC resources were unused or discarded. The *Guardian* newspaper said in August 1993, 'You cannot make a pair of croak-voiced Daleks appear benevolent even if you dress one of them up in an Armani suit and call the other Marmaduke.'[46] This was a reference to John Birt's predilection for Armani and the name of the then Chairman of the Board of Governors, Marmaduke Hussey. Birt's supporters would say that he was justified in dragging the BBC into the digital age.

The issue is not whether change was necessary – it's about how the change was managed. You discard the past at your peril.

It's in the artefacts

We have talked about the past so far as if it's ephemeral, it's in the ether – stories and working practices. But the past lives today also in the physical pieces we preserve. It's like keeping your mum's wedding ring after she dies. If you visit Duke Corporate Education in Durham, North Carolina, you will find the headquarters in the refurbished tobacco warehouse that the Duke family once owned (Duke money originally came from its tobacco business).

This is literally a move back to where it all started and a daily reminder of the business and family heritage. Durham is no longer the centre of the tobacco industry, although it's common to see tobacco leaves ripening for harvesting in people's gardens. (Old habits die hard and they still grow it for personal use. It's in the DNA of the region.)

The old warehouse is on four floors of wide open space, dark wooden floors and beams and giant metal sliding doors. It evokes the past, but also the present. Each area represents a different Duke CE office location. The London area has the road sign for Fleet Street, as well as an intact red phone box.

Hewlett-Packard is also effective at preserving and displaying the past. We'll come to the Hewlett-Packard story later in this chapter. By way of introduction, back in the 1970s, there was a systematic UK government policy to attract inward investment – to encourage overseas companies to set up manufacturing or service bases in the UK. Hewlett-Packard (HP) was one of the companies the government hoped to attract – an iconic, entrepreneurial computer manufacturer from California. (The lure of Silicon Valley has been around longer than you think.)

The Hewlett-Packard executives stood out a mile as they moved from meeting to meeting in Whitehall. It wasn't the neat suits or starched shirts that made them different, but what they wore on their wrists. What looked like big fat watches were multifunctional devices that could act as calculators as well as timekeepers, with a few other functions thrown in too. Sounds pretty basic as you sit there with your iPad, but this was 40 years ago and Japanese miniaturisation had only just started.

Just as Duke University is proud of the family that started it, HP employees are proud of the computer company's founders, Bill Hewlett and Dave Packard. Because of this, they have carefully preserved the original garage where it all started. In fact, in

2005 the corporation spent almost a year returning 367 Addison Avenue to the appearance it would have had in 1939, when the founders, Bill and Dave, founded the now famous Hewlett-Packard partnership. The HP garage is California Historic Landmark No. 976 – the birth of Silicon Valley.

Let go gently

Jasmine Whitbread understands that the future needs to be rooted in the past, not uprooted from it. 'This one stood out for me. That's how I drive forward – there is evidence from the past that makes the case for the next direction going forward. When I joined Save the Children, I looked into the past to chart a way to the future. That's the enterprise, it's a continuum. I am a "passing through" person – it's on my watch.'

But respecting and learning from the past is not the same as safeguarding it at all costs. It also means that you must be capable of letting go of what got you here, if it seems it could hurt the organisation going forwards. All leaders have to integrate dilemmas. This particular dilemma means respecting and integrating the successes of the past, while being ready to let go of your success formula if it constrains the ability to move forward.

An anonymous anecdote may help here. An organisation was wondering how to move forwards and away from the past. They organised a huge internal conference and had designed an event that would involve a physical ceremony representing the past being consigned to history in order to make way for a brave new future. They had company archives carried onto the stage and placed in a huge bin. Luckily the rehearsal was observed by a senior executive, who could scarcely believe the crassness of the gesture. It was quickly reconfigured, so that the archives were not 'binned', but ceremoniously placed in a vault, with the key safeguarded for posterity.

It's perfectly OK to move away from the past, as Nokia has achieved in spectacular fashion. Just do it with respect. Be seen to build on a proud heritage, not trash it. The advice from *no safety net* was not to get too far ahead, in case they think that you are the enemy. The advice here is to bring the past, or a version of it, with you.

> be seen to build on a proud heritage, not trash it

Without its past, the organisation has no solid core.

It's not all about now

The present is a time sink. From the moment our eyes open, we are running to keep up with the slew of communications that besets us.

Modern technology and hand-held devices support a modern obsession with being in touch and up to date with the most recent communication at all times. Email, search, text, blog, twitter – this is the new lexicon of the soundbite mentality. There's a reason we nickname the Blackberry 'crackberry': being in touch is addictive. We are losing the ability to spend time in conversation with others (as opposed to in companionable silence, each communing with our particular choice of electronic device); and we are losing the ability to concentrate.

On an executive development programme in Asia in mid 2010, we confiscated all the hand-held devices. After an initial riot of disapproval, after two days the participants thanked us, for removing the distraction and allowing them to be 'present'.

Technology dulls the brain

There was a delightful article[47] by Nicholas Carr in the Saturday Review section of *The Times*, in which he asks if the

internet is changing the way we think and making us stupid.
He has written a book about this, too.[48] There is plenty of
research to demonstrate that our brains cannot cope with the
constant stimulus of new information and that we operate at
a level of heightened stress on a continuous basis. Because
it's continuous, we fail to notice it. Carr's book summarises
key research. He demonstrates, for example, that the internet
encourages rapid sampling of small bits of information
from many sources – we may, on our surfing journeys, end
up forgetting why we started in the first place. So we are
becoming more adept at scanning, but losing our capacity for
concentration and reflection.

It is not just technology that keeps us in the here and now. It
is also the pressure from the market. As a corporation, you
are only as good as your last quarter's results. As one of my
dear colleagues would say, the prime directive of the CEO is
sustainability, as measured by TSR – Total Shareholder Return.
If your shares are not doing as well as those of competitors, the
sound of institutional shareholders stampeding to market to
sell your shares will be deafening. The next quarter's results are
immediate and imperative. There is no doubt that you have to
spend significant amounts of your attention on the here and now.

This is another leadership dilemma. In the vernacular, would
you like jam today or jam tomorrow? In business speak, do you
want returns today or growth tomorrow? The answer is 'yes'.

Be a nerd

Living in the present is also about really understanding your
organisation and how it works. Whether it's a manufacturing
plant or a charity, you have to know the organisation inside out.
One take on the financial services crisis of 2008 is that there
was much too little focus on the basics of banking, on how the
system actually works. The successful leader has a thorough
understanding of the business, a huge grasp of the intricacies

of the system. When asked a technical question, they often know the answer at length and in detail. As one of the CEOs commented, 'You sweat the small stuff'; another said 'I am a nerd and should probably get out more.'

you have to know the organisation inside out

Keeping strong results coming in, quarter after quarter, is what keeps us inventing management fads on an annual basis. As an executive, have you, for example, looked at Total Quality Management, Just in Time Production techniques, Five Forces strategic analysis, the Seven S Model, Action Learning, Offshoring, Centres of Excellence, Outsourcing, Delayering, Orthodoxies, Co-opetition, Six Sigma, Empowerment – to name just a few? (It's hard to keep up, isn't it?)

It's not that the number of ideas about how to run an organisation has increased or accelerated that dramatically. It's more that a few core ideas are recycled with new titles. It's not just to keep consultants in business either – it's as much about keeping managers engaged and motivated. Don't underestimate the grinding attention to detail that it takes to run a global business. The business consultants' imaginarium is a great way of keeping us all motivated.

So in a sense, worry less about this time zone than the others. There are strong forces at play to keep you heavily engaged in today. Worry more about making time in the diary for the past (a bit) and the future.

No instant gratification

Talking about old ideas with a new label, do you know Daniel Goleman's work on Emotional Intelligence? His book[49] explains the importance of empathy, warmth and understanding others at work (as opposed to just focusing on the task to be completed, or the work itself). This idea was not new (it has been proved over and again in small group research dating back to the 1930s), but it was an important and timely reminder.

From engineers to marshmallows

There is a constant tension in organisations between adhering to sound engineering principles in design and execution, while remembering that organisations actually run because of the people who inhabit them. This tension stems back to the industrial revolution. The most famous consultant of the late nineteenth century was Frederick Winslow Taylor, who used engineering principles to increase productivity dramatically in factories.[50] His fundamental belief was that people were lazy and would take any opportunity they could to slack. He believed that they needed to be controlled by managers, or experts (in the organisational principles he advocated) to get a good day's work out of them.

Psychologists didn't start to play a real role in organisations until the Hawthorne Studies of the 1930s,[51] when we started to take into account that how a person feels about the job – not just how the work is organised – can also affect productivity and morale. (Today, with the advent of neuroscience, cognitive psychology is reinforcing its deserved platform in organisations.)

Can 4-year-olds be patient?

This technical explanation aside, Goleman's work provided a much-needed reminder that it is also possible to get a good day's work out of people through understanding them and their motivations as individuals. In his book, he cites Walter Mischel's research with children and marshmallows. In the late 1960s, Mischel experimented in the 'game room' at Bing Nursery School on the campus of Stanford University. Small children as young as 4 years old were seated in front of a delicacy of their choice (an example being a marshmallow) and encouraged to be patient – not to eat the treat immediately. If they could sit without eating it until the researcher came back into the room (sometimes as long what must have seemed an agonizing 15 minutes), they were rewarded with a second treat.

You can imagine the full range of human behaviour that this elicited. When left alone, some children ate the marshmallow immediately; some visited the tray of treats, which was also left in the room with them, and ate more; some sang, wriggled and distracted themselves so that they could earn the second treat. When Walter Mischel followed up with his 653 children later in life, he found that those who had the patience to wait and to earn a second treat were generally more successful. It's called the ability to delay gratification – to show patience and focus on longer-term gain over immediate satisfaction. It's an incredibly important attribute for a leader.

Redo your calendar

Let's hear again from Dennis Nally, Chairman of the PricewaterhouseCoopers International Network. 'I applaud this research, I can't tell you how right it is. This is about arranging the organisational agenda in order to have quality time to spend on the future – which may not be as gratifying as spending time on the short term, putting out fires and driving results. But you have to spend substantive time positioning for the future, looking at strategic alternatives, where you are not clear what the real benefit is. This means spending as much as 50 per cent of your time on things like developing talent and planning succession, where there is no immediate payback. Yet you must act, redo your calendar to find the time.'

The tyranny of the present

Weeks after the interview, I was struck again by the simplicity of Dennis's very pragmatic idea. And at one level, it is that simple – all you have to do is to make sure that you put time in your calendar that is dedicated to creating the future. If it's in the calendar, it will happen. But he is also commenting on the tyranny of the present. It's very easy to get caught up in today's work. It can feel very rewarding to handle a crisis and emerge a hero.

> put time in your calendar that is dedicated to creating the future

You are the leader because you have deep capability and can see the broader landscape. You find decisions straightforward that others struggle with. There is an adrenalin surge that accompanies fixing something, especially when others can't and they look to you for guidance. Yet ask yourself this. How many of the crises might be prevented with a little forward planning? As one CEO said to me, if you like putting out fires so much, you should join the Fire Brigade.

And lastly, Dennis is giving us some guidance on how much time to spend on the work of the future, whether it's on business or the very important and often overlooked area of talent development. Fifty per cent of your time is a lot, isn't it? Can you reorganise your diary to spend 50 per cent of your time in the future?

Make sure everyone gets the bug

And it's not just about demonstrating the importance of living in the future time zone by doing it yourself, as a role model. It's also about engaging others in the future too. Dennis again: 'Our Network of the Future was led by 14–15 senior leaders, all with big day jobs. We set up forums to engage about the future and include others. The job of the CEO is to create the ambience where this happens. Driving operating results today versus setting a direction towards the future are fundamentally different. The pace of change is so great that if you don't consider the "what ifs" you will be caught looking in the rear view mirror.'

The future is not created by extending the past forwards – or driving through the rear view mirror. The future is created by living there, with all the uncertainty, ambiguity and complexity that this implies. You have to eat, breathe and live in the future – for about half your time.

Living in three time zones

It was a typical scorching day in North Carolina, hot as Hades with 90% humidity, but it was cool and shaded inside. It was the start of a week together learning about leadership and the opening speaker was Blair Sheppard. Blair was still the CEO of Duke CE at the time and would not move on to become the Dean of the Duke Fuqua School of Business for another four years.

Yet the story was somehow telling the story of his future too. It was clear that Blair was a dedicated 'Dookie' (the pronunciation is important, as all 'Dookies' know – not 'u' but 'oo').

Twenty-four mining executives listened attentively as Blair told the story of how the Duke family had used their wealth, founded on the tobacco industry, to create and build Duke University. The story told about the past and the many 'firsts' the Duke family had created. How they had attracted top teaching talent to attract the best students. Their foresight in establishing one of the first (separate, of course) campuses for women alongside the male campus (the two campuses had to be separated by a 10 foot high wall, but six feet of it was in the foundations!). The quarry they bought to source a specific type of stone so that the new buildings could look as old as the one they were modelling it on – the University of Cambridge in the United Kingdom.

Blair then moved on to talk about the University today, with its wealth and breadth of departments and institutes, world-class research and award-winning faculty. The story ended with a look ahead and a view of how the richness of the present would provide the foundation for a bigger global role for Duke University in the future.

It was a seamless story and one that contained a lot of nuggets of leadership advice. And it was an effortless example of a leader at home in three time zones. Reverence for the past. Affection for the present. Aspiration for the future.

A foot in three camps

Dominique Fournier is the CEO of Infineum International Ltd, which formulates, manufactures and markets petroleum additives for lubricants and fuels. It was established in January 1999 as a joint venture of two of the oil company giants, ExxonMobil and Shell. Much smaller than either of its parents (1,600 employees, but still spread across 70 countries and operating in 20 languages), its research base goes back much further than 1999 – almost 80 years. Dominique is Infineum's second CEO and he was appointed in January 2005, joining them from ExxonMobil Chemical in Houston, Texas.

Dominique's driving passion is people (he wants to rename Human Resources as a function, because it's not an exciting title – and because he believes that people don't want to be thought of as 'assets'). He lives his life in three time zones.

'This is a continuum in your mind. You have your two feet in the three moments. At Infineum, we have to remember Shell and Exxon as our roots. The past is the engine for progress and too much energy is dissipated because we lose the lessons from the past. Yet, I have always believed that a lot of the future lies in the present – if we could only read the signals.'

No jetlag

As we have learnt to expect from our CEOs, the way they see it and how they do it are as individual as they are. What they have in common is how they think. And they think in three time zones. Clive Bannister sees it as social insight. 'There are four aspects to working effectively with executive colleagues: empathy (the ability to get on with other people); forward-looking radar (to see what is coming); experience and history (know what is going on); the ability to know what others need today and to compromise (and not see this as failure).' There are our three time zones – forward, history and today – with empathy as the bond.

John Tusa expresses it in a different way. 'At the World Service (I left there in 1993) I spent a fair amount of time reminding people of its history and relating it to today and showing continuity. I am an historian. I spend about 50 per cent of my time on the present, but only as a way of knitting it all together and linking it to the future.'

Different nationalities see time differently

Do you remember the simple time management exercise earlier in the chapter? When asked to draw three circles representing the past, present and future, Western executives tend to draw three separate circles, arranged in a line from left to right, past, present and future, in that order. With Americans, the circle representing the future tends to be larger. It's a different story in the East. The Chinese, for example, draw the circles inside each other. The past, present and future are, in some sense, one.[52] How do you live in three time zones at the same time? How do you remember the past, spend some time on today's business, and focus on building the future? Maybe you have to be Chinese.

It's more than just legacy

Thoughtful leaders do think about the legacy that they will leave behind. What does this mean? Just like a person who has built up wealth over time plans ahead on how to pass the wealth on to others in a will, so leaders are purposeful about what will be left after they depart. (The key difference is that, unless you are unlucky, your departure will be to a fulfilling retirement, rather than death.) Whether it is a more prosperous business, greater global reach, a new way of working, a contribution to reducing the impact of climate change – a leader often wants to be able to point to a specific achievement that leaves the enterprise in a better position.

> leaders are purposeful about what will be left after they depart

There has been increasing discussion about leadership legacy over the past decade. It pre-dated the 2008 financial services crisis, but was exacerbated by it. With so many apparently invincible companies failing during the crisis, like Lehman Brothers which declared bankruptcy in 2008, the emphasis on a leader leaving behind a strong and prosperous legacy was brought into even sharper focus.

And it's a good thing for leaders to worry about what they leave behind as they depart – hopefully, an organisation in good shape with talented people to run it. We have always wanted more from our leaders than charisma. The danger with charisma is that it is entrancing in the moment, but too often the charismatic figure leaves too big a hole behind, with little in the way of systems and processes for enduring success.

So 'my legacy' is certainly a positive outlook. It means that the executive is thinking about the future and the time when she or he will have left the organisation. But it's not the only time zone to devote time to.

It also suggests that the leader is looking for the one, possibly heroic, act that will ensure a place in the history books. *On my watch* is more about quiet stewardship towards a successful future for all.

Stewards in the moment

We talked about the tremendous uncertainty that faced the future of Alico in Chapter 2, as AIG worked to pay back the US government for its bailout in 2008. It was a story about navigating the enterprise in uncharted waters. What I hadn't realised, until Chairman and CEO Rod Martin rang me on 1 November (the day that AIG's successful sale of Alico to MetLife, Inc for just over $16 billion was announced), was how much his story was also about stewardship.

Rod was excited, happy, relieved and ebullient on the phone – a whole range of emotions triggered by the successful end to their two-year journey. He had two big pieces of news: that this would launch a much enhanced global company, and that most of the employees at Alico were to keep their jobs going forwards – unlike him. 'One of the most challenging pieces of the last six months has been the knowledge that I and most of my executive team are not part of the go-forward story. We retire from AIG today (apart from a transition period to MetLife). We worked very hard to finish it properly. The baton has been passed.'

Rod sent a personal letter of thanks to all 12,000 employees, in 17 different languages. He was touched by how many replied. He told me: 'I feel a personal sense of ownership and accountability as the steward of a 90-year heritage and, second, as the "keeper of the flame" to realise Alico's aspiration to be a world leader.' He safeguarded the past, managed through the crisis, and launched the future.

By the way, are you wondering why Rod rang me on his 'day of days'? After all, he had plenty of other important business to keep him occupied. It was because I told him it was the deadline for getting the manuscript to the publisher and he wanted to help. His generosity of spirit is humbling.

On my watch is a gracious way of thinking. It implies that the leader has the humility to know that she or he is one in a line of leaders and that the task is to accept, and to pass on, the baton seamlessly. It acknowledges the time zones – that you pick up from your predecessors, who managed the past, to you in the present. And, at the end of your time, you have to pass it on to someone else to lead the future. Even if your time is curtailed by unexpected events – in Rod's case, a crisis of survival – you have to leave the place in good shape. So you try new ventures to keep the organisation current, but you don't bet the farm – or sleep at the wheel.

Try it for yourself. Think *on my watch*. Does it feel like a more authentic way to think about your role than dwelling just on the legacy that you will leave behind?

What if you fail?

If you can't think in this way, at a personal level, you might of course lose your job. We've already talked about the Hewlett-Packard garage as a visible artefact of HP's DNA. Let's pick this story up again.

The public story of former CEO and Chairman of Hewlett-Packard, Carly Fiorina, is a really interesting and complex example.

Some facts are not contested. She was the CEO and Chairman of HP from 1999 to 2005. In 2002, the company completed a contentious merger with rival computer company Compaq, under her leadership. It was widely reported in the press at the time that board member Walter Hewlett (son of the company co-founder William (Bill) Hewlett) opposed the bid and it is common knowledge that he led an (unsuccessful) proxy fight against it. In 2005, Carly was ousted by the Board.

Carly was, and is, a very successful woman, who stood for election as a Republican candidate in the 2010 US election, hoping to represent California in the Senate. In 1998, while she was still at Lucent, *Fortune* magazine named her as 'the most powerful woman in business' in its inaugural listing. She was included in the Time 100 in 2004 and stayed in the Fortune listing throughout her time at HP. She was number 10 on the *Forbes* magazine list of the World's 100 Most Powerful Women in 2004. She was the first woman to lead a Fortune 20 company. The pedigree is extraordinary.

Here is where opinion divides – dramatically. In 2008, Infoworld grouped her with a list of products and ideas that had flopped,[53] saying that she was the 'anti-Steve Jobs' for reversing the good will of American engineers (or 'geeks' as they called them) and alienating existing customers. On the other hand, in the same year, the *New York Times* ran an article[54] which said that the EDS acquisition by HP in 2008 was evidence that Fiorina had the right strategy 'regardless of the turmoil she brought to HP'. (Fiorina had proposed this acquisition in 2000, but dropped the idea after it received a poor reception from HP shareholders.)

In April 2009, the business magazine web site Condé Nast Portfolio listed Fiorina as one of the 20 'worst American CEOs of all time', citing the HP–Compaq merger as a failure. They also quoted the halving of HP's stock value under Fiorina's tenure and suggested that she was a self-publicist who paid herself handsomely, while laying off thousands of workers.

If you believe Fiorina herself, she claims that 'the controversial merger with Compaq Computer is now acknowledged to be the most successful merger in high-tech history and positioned HP to become the first $100 billion information technology company, creating market leadership positions for the company in every one of its product lines'.[55]

She failed to take the past with her

This is one of those stories where we need to agree to disagree. But let's look one layer down. Whatever she did or didn't do; whatever she did or didn't say, she failed to take Walter Hewlett with her. And Walter Hewlett represented the past, the family name, the proud heritage. Fiorina may have been right in her strategy, but that's not the point. Look back to Chapter 3, where we talk about how, when the data says the call is 49/51, there is no 'right' answer – there is only the decision that you can persuade most people to follow. The decision where you know you have successfully persuaded them to labour alongside you to make it work.

Over a decade on, and this remarkable woman is still having to justify the actions that helped to put HP ahead of Dell.

A final thought

We can't predict the behaviours you will see to indicate that the leader thinks in this way. The behaviours will vary as widely as the personalities of the individual leaders. We have seen that already with the stories of the leaders in this chapter.

What we can predict is that if you think in this way, others will be willing to engage and commit to the journey with you, because you will have shown that you understand the history and past successes, and their importance in shaping the future. The heritage will feel safe in your hands and you will simultaneously manage to keep people focused on the here and now, the importance of daily results. You will acknowledge that effort so far is well spent, and the effort today is an important foundation for what we do (and for what those who come after us will do) in the future.

Your watch will be a good one.

Developing *on my watch* thinking: self assessment

If you want to think *on my watch*, consider the following questions as a quick self assessment:

▌ Do you consciously think about three time zones? Do you respect and integrate the history of the organisation? When you move to change business, do people follow you because they know that you respect the past that they created?

▌ Can you deal with the tyranny of the present, without being enslaved to it? Can you avoid getting trapped into constant crisis management? Can you live without the executive 'high' of firefighting?

▌ Do you spend enough time thinking about the future? Can you delay gratification and sacrifice instant reward so that you can build the future? Can you leave the path that got the organisation to where it is today and adopt a different and better route forwards?

▌ Can you juggle living in three time zones and not get jetlag? Can you integrate three time horizons as you tell the stories that explain the heritage of the organisation and what makes the present work well, and encourage others to join you in a different future?

▌ Can you think about your tenure of leadership as fleeting and temporary? Can you accept and pass the baton of leadership seamlessly, from and to the former and next generation of leaders? Do you worry less about your legacy and more about your stewardship?

I am the enterprise

And so to the final way of thinking – although remember that the five don't happen in any particular order. It depends on you.

Where are you now as a leader? As an effective senior executive, you focus on achieving your targets. You understand exactly how your organisation operates. You know where you should and shouldn't tread, where the skeletons are hidden and the frustrations are felt. You use this information to make sure that you co-operate well with colleagues and that they co-operate with you. It means that business gets done, there are no stalemates and everyone moves carefully forwards together. You scratch my back and I'll scratch yours and in the meantime, we deliver results. Your results matter to you and so they should. As one of the major players in the organisation, if you don't deliver, everyone suffers.

think beyond the zero sum game

The next step is to think beyond the zero sum game. It's about more than just your results, it's about how the enterprise as a whole is doing. You have to live it. Sometimes, it might be better for the whole if you didn't deliver your targets, but placed the resources somewhere else, where they might do more good. And you identify so closely with the whole enterprise that people can't tell you apart. You think *I am the enterprise.*

The beginning is the end

Originally, this was supposed to be the opening chapter of the book. As interview followed interview, though, it just seemed too hard a place to start the conversation. And that's because leadership starts with me, the individual, and only then builds into the bigger picture.

If you like, this chapter is about the responsibilities of serving as a leader, the consequences of taking on that huge job and the way you need to think to make a success of it. After 25 years of teaching and consulting on leadership, there was a big surprise for me in this chapter.

Matryoshka doll

You know the Russian nesting doll? I can't think of a better analogy for this way of thinking. As you'll see in this chapter, these leaders live, embody and represent their organisations – there is no separating them. Cut them open and the same values run inside them at every layer, like the name of an English seaside town runs through the pink stick of rock you buy on the pier. Open up the enterprise and there is the leader, nestling neatly inside – a smaller replica of the bigger whole.

There are several aspects to *I am the enterprise*. The first is that you represent the organisation to so many people, both inside and outside the enterprise, that you have to be highly self aware and manage the person that others see. You must be the leader that they need. The second aspect brought the surprise – the strength and depth of the feeling these leaders have for their organisations – they really identify with them. There were many expressions of these feelings in the interviews – passion, conviction, commitment and tears. Leaders believe in, and nurture, the enterprise they lead.

Third, the enterprise is bigger than any individual, even the leader who embodies it so well. The notion is that you can mould the enterprise a little, and contribute to it as much as possible, but its own life force will be stronger and longer lived than your own. As the leader, you make a contribution, but it's one amongst many. Next comes the proposition that it is harder if you are appointed from outside the organisation, because you don't know it so well. If you come in from outside, in order to be effective, you have to make a special effort to establish the same level of identity with the enterprise as someone who has spent a career there.

the enterprise is bigger than any individual

Lastly, when things go wrong, you need to be prepared to step forwards and take the blame. It doesn't matter whether you caused the problem or not; you represent the organisation, something went wrong, and you have to accept the responsibility – without complaint. As Niall FitzGerald, the Deputy Chairman of Thomson Reuters, puts it, 'leaders are lauded and richly rewarded because of the exaggerated levels of accountability that they hold. This is a two-way street. If it goes wrong, you have to stand up and apologise.'

I am the enterprise may well be the hardest way of thinking, because this is where the sacrifices are the biggest. See what you think as you read on.

We start with the idea that, as a leader, you need to embody the enterprise that you want other people to see.

Always on

We haven't heard from Irene Dorner, the President and CEO of HSBC Bank USA, since Chapter 2. Let's return to her story, from the time when she was still running HSBC in Malaysia in 2008.

As the car dropped us at the gate of the house in the sultry Malaysian night, the residence was looking truly ambassadorial. There were two guards at the gatehouse and they rang the house to check that we were on the list. Only then were gates opened and we were allowed to pass by them and climb the steep winding path to the house itself. It was simple, yet elegant, and a riot of colour and noise.

The whole of the ground floor was public space, designed for entertainment and business; the private apartments were upstairs. Locals, in brightly coloured traditional clothes, were playing their classical instruments in a delightful cacophony of noise. The canangs tinkled as they were struck with mallets and the women sat cross-legged and swayed in time to the geduk drums. Each instrument was a pair, with a larger ibu (parent) and a smaller anak (child).

The guests were mingling and relaxing. The CEO and her husband greeted every guest personally at the door and made each and every one feel extraordinarily welcome. Irene moved from group to group, animated and chatting. Her energy was palpable and her enthusiasm contagious. Everything about her leadership was just as she had described it in her interview. She was 'on'.

'You have to manage yourself constantly and look as if everything is okay ALL the time, it's essential for staff. Even my driver, the bedrock of my life, cannot read me. You cannot be Eeyore in face or words; you have to look happy and confident.'

She certainly looked the part as she organised drinks, then dinner, for the executives on the programme we were running in Kuala Lumpur. Irene was the in-country CEO for HSBC and so the visitors were keen to understand her view of the business. She dealt straightforwardly with every question she was asked, always managing to sound upbeat and optimistic. Nothing at all like Eeyore, the depressed donkey from A.A. Milne's *Winnie the Pooh* stories.

It's hard work

The bad news is that this level of commitment takes a lot of hard work. To quote one CEO, 'If you are worried about work/ life balance, I don't need to worry about you getting my job.' As Thomas Edison[56] famously phrased it, genius is 1 per cent inspiration, 99 per cent perspiration. Less famously, he also said: 'Many of life's failures are people who did not realize how close they were to success when they gave up.'[57] This is a charter for hard work and endurance.

It takes energy

'You have to pump energy into that level of understanding; being in control and understanding yourself at all times. My constant priority is, how do I make myself every day focus my talents on being the CEO. Who I am, what I am doing. The second I get in the car I am "on". What of me do I need to contribute to this situation, to make it work, having already thought about it ahead? Learn fast, how to do it well, do it differently.'

It's great to kick off with this energetic quote from Irene. What is she telling us? That part of *I am the enterprise* is being switched on to the role at all times. There can be no space between her and the enterprise. It's more than a representational role, it is as if she embodies it. She gives it a face and a voice. She faithfully represents its hopes, outlook and aspirations. She is the enterprise. So if Irene looks worried, we must be in trouble – right?

Imagine that you are hiring and you have two candidates in the room. One is Irene – upbeat, energetic, optimistic. The other candidate, let's call him Neil, looks worried and a bit depressed. It's obvious that life has kicked Neil around and he hasn't always been on the winning side. He is a bit subdued, a bit wary. Irrespective of their experience and talent, which one are you most drawn towards hiring? (By the way, it would be perverse if you opted for Neil.)

It's the same with organisations. Do you want to work for the buzzy place that appears to be going somewhere – or for the slightly tired place that somehow feels as if its best days are behind it? And it's the leader who sets the tone.

Conscious self-management

People are great boss-watchers. How you look, if you're smiling, whether you are tense or relaxed and confident, makes an impression. We met Tom Albanese, CEO of the global mining group Rio Tinto, in Chapter 3, talking about taking decisions in extreme uncertainty. Here he adds an interesting thought. Tom always looks relaxed and confident. But when they were in the middle of the hostile takeover bid from BHP Billiton, in 2007–2008, he had to advise his executive assistant to be very aware of how she looked too. Because even if Tom looked relaxed, if she looked worried, people assumed that she had just heard something worrying from Tom!

So Irene focuses hard on what she needs to bring to the situation. This short story tells us that leadership is a very conscious act.[58] We say that you need to 'manage yourself so that you can lead others'. Irene is clearly doing that. Even those closest to her cannot guess her real mood. She is self conscious about her leadership and throws all the energy she can into it.

Niall FitzGerald, himself an ebullient optimist for whom 'being on' is not difficult, trains other leaders to do this. He tells talented people 'I am going to give you a challenge that you can't possibly complete. Your real challenge is not to complain about this, or anything else, in the next 24 hours.' This is so simple and so effective – a master class in positive outlook. His summary is typically lyrical: 'Pain is inevitable, misery is optional. The shadow you cast as a leader sets the mood for the whole enterprise.'

It's a symbiotic relationship

If you scuba dive, you've probably seen those pretty little clownfish, dancing in and out of the fronds of an anemone. A clownfish is territorial and sticks close to its chosen anemone. The clownfish protects the anemone from fish that might eat it and the stinging tentacles of the anemone protect the clownfish from its predators. A mutually beneficial relationship – one could not live without the other. And they depend on each other. In biological terms, symbiosis means close and often long-term interactions between different biological species.

> one could not live without the other

This was the surprise. In educating leaders, it is common to talk about being a good role model for others. This is so much more. These leaders feel much more than just strong identification with the values of the enterprise. There is a sense of being the organisation – living it. It's a symbiotic relationship.

You'll hear this sentiment over and over again in the stories in this chapter. Let's reflect on the meaning that we just heard in Irene's story. Without a trace of self-sacrifice, she told us that she looks at every situation and thinks, what does it need now? What do I need to bring to make this work, to make this better? Who do I need to be? How can I set the example that will move us forwards? There is a symbiotic relationship between her and the enterprise; they are as one.

Does this sound extreme? You'll hear it again. This is how leaders think.

Obsession

The strength of feeling is so strong that it's almost an obsession. The job absorbs you.

Vittorio Colao has been the chief executive of Vodafone Group for two years, since 2008. Vodafone has 79,000 employees distributed around the world and in 2010, despite it being known as a mobile telephony business, a third of its revenues already come from non-mobile voice business. Colao brings experience from both inside and outside Vodafone to his role. From 2004 to 2006, he was CEO of RCS MediaGroup in Milan, which publishes newspapers, magazines and books in Italy, Spain and France. Prior to RCS, he held other jobs in Vodafone, before returning in 2006. He describes three formative experiences in his life: military school, where he learnt about the power of unlimited energy and unlimited possibilities; McKinsey, which taught him the value of honest, thorough, clinical analysis of facts; and joining Vodafone, an exciting, entrepreneurial company.

Colao freely admits to obsession, on a number of fronts, from the strategic to the operational. 'I am obsessed. I am convinced that Vodafone is going to make it, but each of the three pieces of our transition is very challenging and has its own issues in the future. My obsession is, how do I best help Vodafone make a profitable evolution into a leading provider of "total communications"? I am obsessed with having the best products, giving the best experience to the customers, and doing it in a profitable way for the shareholders. I once noticed that one of our airport shops was closed at 6.15 in the morning and next door there were three shops open; so I immediately questioned our choice. You must really be obsessed with performance and delivering service to the customers.'[59]

living the enterprise happens from the inside out

This is more than just a job to Colao. Living the enterprise happens from the inside out. Like *solid core*, it becomes part of your DNA, so much a part of you that it is essentially unconscious. It is who you are. For external and internal stakeholders you are the enterprise. You cannot have a point of view different from the enterprise's. You can't have a bad day. You always speak as the leader.

And when you talk to the people who work for these leaders, this is exactly what they want to see; not personal ambition, but an intensity and commitment to make the enterprise prosper.

Live the place

Richard Fleck CBE was first mentioned in Chapter 3, 'Comfortable in discomfort'. Herbert Smith is a legal practice that has grown from 4 to 14 offices and from about 100 to 2,500 personnel since Richard first joined them. Having been a partner with the firm from 1980, Richard was actively involved in developing the firm's strategy and then led the practice over this period. He currently works as a consultant with Herbert Smith, as well as being a director of the Financial Reporting Council, Chairman of the Auditing Practices Board, Chairman of the Consultancy and Advisory Group to the International Ethical Standards Board for Accountants and non-executive Director of the National Audit Office. (As he says, 'I have always over-traded!' – he works very hard.)

Richard's is one of the many stories that there was no space to cover in Chapter 2, 'No safety net', but he is widely credited with taking Herbert Smith international, from a strong UK base, over this period. Richard ticks many of the boxes we have come to expect from our leaders: exceptionally smart, very dedicated, an optimist who can count on the fingers of one hand the nights he hasn't been able to sleep because of worrying about the business – and someone with buckets of energy. *I am the enterprise* caught his attention first in the interview.

'*I am the enterprise* is the fundamental truth. As a leader, you have to care passionately about the organisation. If you care deeply and you can communicate that, it is inspirational.

You have a deep understanding, and you are in tune with the enterprise. There were a total of 100 people in the firm when I joined; we now have 2,500 around the world. This has been quite a journey.'

Richard has spent his life working in and building the practice. There is no space between him and it. Even when, in 2005, his partners did not choose him to lead them in an internal election – a close-run disappointment after so many years of dedication – he remained committed. He is known in legal circles as 'Mr Herbert Smith'. You can't get much closer to the enterprise than that.

Love the place

We first met Ronnie Leten, CEO of the engineering company Atlas Copco, in Chapter 2. The company has been in business for 130 years and manufactures and distributes compressors, generators, construction and mining equipment and industrial tools all over the world – in 174 countries. It has its headquarters in Stockholm, Sweden, and has 76 production facilities in 20 countries, the largest being in Belgium, Sweden, Germany, Italy, the United States, India and China. Its annual revenue is roughly 70 million Swedish krona and it employs more than 30,000 people.

Ronnie has a similar story to Richard Fleck, except that he did have to leave Atlas Copco for a period. He first joined the company in 1985 and left in 1996 after failing to get an internal promotion for which he had been encouraged to apply. He didn't leave because he didn't get the job – it was the way the company dealt with the aftermath.

We were working on a development programme for Atlas Copco executives in Putrajaya, the new administrative centre of the Federal Government of Malaysia, in a hotel right next to the King's Palace. The value that Ronnie places on development became even clearer during our four days there. Not only did he dedicate all his time to us, interacting with the participants and leading the strategy sessions – he also sat individually with participants to talk to them about next steps in their career journey. He is warm and inclusive – he would phone other mentors and supporters to include them during the conversations too.

I had to leave

He talked about the time when he felt compelled to leave the company. Paradoxically, they didn't want him to leave and his boss even refused to sign his resignation letter. It was a stressful time at home as well – his wife and he were both working and the children were small.

'No-one who had encouraged me to apply for the job talked to me about why I didn't get it. I received no feedback. It was a violation of my principles – you need to take care of people.' A headhunter found Ronnie a local job with less travel and more money – and he was miserable. After 25 years in Atlas Copco employees receive a golden pin in acknowledgement of their service and they join the Gold Club reunions. Even at the age of 35, after only 11 years of service, such was his loyalty to the company he was upset to think that he would never receive this pin of long service.

The company kept in touch and immediately started the process of wooing him back. He returned to Atlas Copco in 1997 and was appointed CEO in January 2009. Even now, he finds the memory of his departure painful. 'I found the transition to working outside Atlas Copco harder than I found the transition into this CEO role. I like to think that I didn't really leave, but was on a special training assignment for a year.'

As with Richard Fleck, there is a happy ending. 'I just heard that I will get my golden pin at the end of October. The day they told me, I had to go into my office and be alone for a while to let the news sink in.' It is apparent in his voice and tone how much the award means to him. Then, with a characteristic twinkle, he added 'but I am married with my wife'.

Ronnie's story is possibly the clearest, but represents the same sentiment encountered with our other leaders. The leader's role is much more than representational; the organisation and the individual are intertwined.

Selflessness

Jasmine Whitbread of Save the Children was equally direct. 'I do embody the values of Save the Children. But I am not the enterprise. The enterprise is much bigger than me. Everything you do must be for the organisation.'

> you put yourself second, at the exact same moment when you have all the power

Giving to something that you acknowledge is bigger than you, without expecting credit, is selfless. Don't we all like to be acknowledged for our contribution? 'Everything you do must be for the organisation.' That sounds like a lot of sacrifice. It means that you put yourself second, at the exact same moment when you have all the power. It means that you are constantly alert and checking what the situation needs from you. You want to do your best for the organisation, when sometimes it may not be the best for you.

For some CEOs it is not just about doing what the enterprise needs. It goes beyond that and they are trying to contribute on an even greater scale. This can be found most often in the best CEOs who work in emerging economies, where they know that nation building is supported by creating wealth through running a successful business.

Sim Tshabalala: 'Banking is not just about making money. I believe that this is only one of the things we do. We are an organ of society, we mobilise the resources of society for productive investment and we are answerable to everybody in society who provides those resources.'

Sim gives what it takes to be the Deputy CEO of the Standard Bank group and he is also willing to go further. He will give more support to help build the society around it. In his case, selflessness goes beyond the borders of the enterprise into society.

It's bigger than you

As Jasmine says, 'the enterprise is much bigger than me'. She was not the only one to express this sentiment. Let's return to Jacko Maree for a moment. He expounds on his idea that he is at one with the enterprise. 'People describing me would say that I understand Standard Bank, I love Standard Bank, I am passionate about what it stands for and what I am going to do. It is my reason for being (other than home). I absorb and immerse myself in the culture and help to shape it, but only on the edges, because it is bigger than I am.'

'It is bigger than I am.' On the surface, this is a statement of the obvious. The Standard Bank Group employs over 40,000 people, so, yes, bigger than one person, even if that one person is the CEO. Ask yourself a more interesting question. What is the nuance in 'I absorb myself in the culture and help to shape it, but only on the edges'?

Think again about the power of the global CEO, who can command and move resources around the world. The lifestyle of the leader, who always needs to be somewhere in the world, doing something. The conference in Shanghai, the town hall address in Dubai, the investor meeting in London. A thousand tugs on the sleeve every day.

You can't control it

Sometimes it can get like a spy novel. All the sanitised versions of life at the top, with the steely-eyed leader alert and capable and in control, are somewhat illusory. It gets messy.

If you are engaged in big takeover or merger talks, more than one government is likely to be interested in the outcome. You might find your phone being tapped, your conversations recorded and your movements shadowed. As you take the jet or the helicopter to the next meeting, so that you can be met by the car to whisk you off to the following event and you are briefed in the car by the Ambassador, because of the political implications of investing in this country … well, you get the picture. It can be heady.

And you see your name and your photo in the press regularly and sometimes the world seems focused just on getting you ready for the next presentation, the next decision, the next encounter. Every human being sees the world from the centre of their own little universe. The CEO universe is one where the centrifugal force of being 'me' can give the leader an inflated sense of self. Can you see how it might go to your head?

So Jacko's view is refreshing. He loves the organisation he represents, but he doesn't let his robust ego trick him into believing that he is more important than it. He is cautious about how he represents it. He knows that his tenure will shape it, but 'only at the edges'. He's in charge but not in control. He wants to represent it faithfully; to affect it slightly; but to remember that it is bigger than him and not his to own or shape completely.

The troublesome 'I'

Some of these leaders shied away from this simple pronoun – the 'I' in *I am the enterprise*. There was a concern that it sounded too egotistical. So some of them paused over this one. They wanted to acknowledge that they led with others, not alone.

We met Dominique Fournier, the CEO of Infineum, in the previous chapter. He hesitated here. 'I spend a lot of my time trying to make the company better – not for me, but for the company. So I agree with "I am the enterprise". But I don't like the flipside – the iconisation of the job. My perfect image of leadership is the orchestra. The leader chooses the symphony and how it will be played – and people talk about the conductor, but the orchestra also has a famous name. Everything is not because of me.'

Niall FitzGerald was similarly reluctant. 'This is too personalised. I am the custodian. I'd like it to say on my tombstone that I found and developed talent that was better than me.'

Another chairman said: 'I back away from this one; it's not how you lead a sports team or any other kind of team. Maybe it's how you run the business in a short-term crisis.'

These reactions fit well with the section on humility from Chapter 4, 'Solid core'. Leadership has many paradoxes and this is one of them. Each in their own way, these leaders are strong characters, with firm opinions and transparent values. They don't hesitate to state a view or make a decision. Yet at the same time, they see themselves doing all this in service of the enterprise. So they don't want the stories to be about them, but about enterprise achievements.

They tend towards self-deprecating comments in the interviews. For example, one said: 'This is a bit about me, so I apologise for that.' Another said 'I never believed I could be a model for anybody'. More than one offered to rephrase the name for this way of thinking. Jacko Maree suggested, 'I agree with all the statements underneath it. Could you call it *I am at one with the enterprise?*' And of course, his instinct is right. The sentiment underpinning the phrase is that you and the enterprise are indistinguishable – you represent it faithfully, in good times and in bad.

And every time I thought about it, I kept coming back to the Matryoshka doll.

Leadership isn't about a straightforward, easy path to success, either personal or organisational. It's about courage and setbacks, a willingness to take chances and to be accountable for the consequences. It's a roller coaster ride with highs and lows. Core roles include Cat Herder, coaxing a wide range of stakeholders to face in the same direction, and Chief Anarchist, leading change. There is an 'I'.

In the end, this title is worth the debate it provokes.

You can't hide behind the team

If we look ahead to the BP story (see page 162), think of the reaction if Tony Hayward had said 'it's not me, it's the team' or 'it was a team decision'. We would have howled with derision. It's you that the Board calls to account, that the shareholders demand be fired, that the employees watch to test if everything is going well.

We wanted his 'I' on the line. No hiding place, no space for the team, no 'we'.

Coming in from outside

Do you remember Kevin Kelly, the global CEO of Heidrick & Struggles? As someone who finds, places and nurtures CEO and board talent, his perspective here is really valuable.

'CEOs who come in from the outside and dismiss all that has gone before end up struggling. I have seen it backfire. In Asia, expats come in and declare that the corporate and the culture are screwed up. I know everything doesn't work, but you can't dismiss it all.'

Vittorio Colao, CEO of Vodafone, agrees. 'It's much more difficult when you come from the outside, because when you come from another firm, you are totally clueless about where people are and what they are thinking, because you haven't seen and worked with them before.'[60]

There is a definite sequencing needed here. Part of landing well, being effective if you come in from outside the organisation, is to become the enterprise, before you can move it forwards. In France, new CEOs do nothing for six months. Today, it is common for incoming CEOs to plan their first 100 days.

Become the enterprise

The advice here is, take some time to become the enterprise before you do anything. Let the people you are about to lead feel comfortable that you get it, believe in it and live it – or you won't be successful in changing what needs to be changed.

Sir Stuart Rose started his working life as a trainee with Marks & Spencer, where he stayed from 1972 until 1989, when he left to join Debenhams.[61] After a successful career in retailing and having earned a reputation as an expert at turnarounds, he re-joined Marks & Spencer as CEO in 2004, after a gap of 15 years. M&S were struggling and Rose is credited with restoring them to greatness within 2 years. Clearly, it was an effective entry. How did he do it?

He is quoted as saying 'You know, I never doubted for a second the brand was capable of reorganisation. Listen, there's nobody, if they're a retailer, who wouldn't want to be chief executive of Marks & Spencer. It's an iconic job – one of the best in the land.'[62]

Imagine you are one of the 85,000 people working in Marks & Spencer at this time. The new CEO clearly loves the retail business and has spent his working life in it. And he lauds M&S as an icon, the one place that anyone in retail would die to lead. Would you feel reassured? Would you believe that he understood the place and wanted the very best for its future? Would you follow him?

The same values

Sir Stuart says more: 'We're simple shopkeepers whose job is to satisfy customers. It has been about ... five words that describe what we do: quality, value, service, innovation and trust. I dusted those words off when I came in 2004.'[63]

This short quote resonates with so many other parts of this explanation about how a CEO thinks. It reminds us of Jasmine Whitbread's story in Chapter 4, as she set about finding that the values of the Save the Children organisation were the same as hers. It reminds us of Jacko Maree, earlier in this chapter, acknowledging that the leader is just one person and that the enterprise is bigger. But more than anything else, this quote tells us that Rose was able to 'dust off' and adopt for himself core values held by the organisation.

He became M&S – then he lost no time in turning it around (two years is pretty fast, by anyone's standards).

Imbibe the DNA

The message here is that Rose spent time imbibing the DNA, before he moved on to his change agenda.

Remember the story of Gerstner's turnaround of IBM in Chapter 5? One of the things that Gerstner said at the time was about the culture. Recall that this was his first time at IBM, where he was enormously successful as a leader. 'Underneath all the sophisticated processes, there is always the company's sense of values and identity. It took me to age 55 to figure that out. The thing I have learnt at IBM is that culture is everything.'[64]

One of the reasons that Gerstner was successful as a newcomer to IBM, which had an exceptionally strong culture, was that he understood how important it was for him to own it, before he could move it forwards. He spent time getting to know it, understand it, praise it and live it. So even rank outsiders can 'become' the enterprise. It just takes insight, time and patience to do so. We started to talk about this in Chapter 5, 'On my watch' – celebrating the past. This takes us one step further than acknowledging the past. It's how you make it your own, when you are coming in from the outside.

How do you immerse yourself and learn to love the place? Leaders drive change, they sense the right thing to do and they want to get on with the job. How do you hold on to all that passion and intensity and still take enough time to prove how much you value the enterprise first, so that you can be more effective in the long run?

Take it on the chin

'The buck stops here' is a phrase that was popularised by US President Harry S. Truman – he had the words inscribed on a sign that he kept on his desk in the Oval Office.[65] When you see press stories about giant organisations, whether good or bad, it is the CEO's name that is quoted. The leader represents the organisation and, fairly or unfairly, this is the name that we see, talk about and quote. That's where the buck stops. So when it goes wrong, you have to be prepared to take it on the chin.

It wasn't Citi that was said to have failed customers and investors, it was Sandy Weill. It wasn't IBM that got the credit for turning itself around in the 90s, it was Lou Gerstner. It wasn't BP that got blamed for polluting the shores of the Mexican Gulf, it was Tony Hayward. It wasn't CISCO that was said to have survived the dot-com bubble, it was John Chambers. The premium placed on leadership is immense. It's how Warren Buffett builds his fortunes: he invests in companies where he likes the leadership. All these leaders love their enterprises – but sometimes, it goes wrong.

Then, the buck stops and it's sometimes really painful. Your job as a leader, when things go wrong, is to step forwards and take it. It may not be fair or right – but that's the price you pay to get the part.

Let's think about the BP story. Or, more appropriately, the Tony Hayward story. He was more pragmatic than you might expect after losing his CEO position of 3 years and his career of 28 years at BP. He said: 'This is a very sad day for me personally. Whether it is fair or unfair is not the point. I became the public face (of the disaster) ... BP cannot move on in the US with me as its leader ... Life isn't fair.'[66]

it matters little whether events feel fair or not

He makes a strong point, doesn't he? In life, it matters little whether events feel fair or not. The fact is that he knows that BP cannot move forwards as long as he is in charge. The personal campaign against him was just too vitriolic. So he was resigned to leaving, so that BP could recover.

The BP story

The story is dramatic and well known. On 20 April 2010, the Deepwater Horizon oil rig exploded, killing 11 workers. The oil rig was licensed to BP, drilling for the Macondo project 5,000 feet below sea level. It was, until the disaster, an outstanding feat of engineering to drill at this depth. The remaining 115 workers were evacuated from the rig the next day and it collapsed into the sea the day after, producing a 5 mile long oil slick.

The well's blowout preventer failed and so oil started leaking into the Gulf of Mexico. President Obama himself came in for criticism, for not visiting the site until 2 May. He pledged resources to contain the spill, but maintained strongly that it was BP's responsibility. On 10 May, BP gained permission to spray chemicals on the spill while making ongoing attempts to create relief wells and cap the spill. On 26 May, BP started its 'top kill' operation to close the well, which worked by 16 July and was confirmed as successful on 4 August.

On 27 July, Hayward stepped down as Chief Executive, to be replaced by American Bob Dudley. BP reported its first quarterly loss in 18 years and set aside a fund of $20.8 billion to pay for the clean-up operation.

It didn't matter that Hayward may not personally have taken the decision to drill in the Gulf. It was irrelevant that the rig was licensed, not owned or operated, by BP. This was BP's problem and therefore Tony Hayward's accountability.

Couldn't get much worse, could it? Can you imagine what it felt like to be in Hayward's shoes? He was never a showman or a big public face for BP, until the disaster pushed him into the limelight. And then this rather thoughtful geologist, who tried to answer questions and accusations factually, sometimes said the wrong thing. Out of the hundreds of hours of interviews, maybe three or four times he made an inappropriate remark. In the information-crazy twenty-first century, that handful of remarks received more coverage and repetition than the hundreds of appropriate remarks he made.

It's not about fairness

He's a decent bloke, hard-working, a good family man – and like Jasmine Whitbread, he's probably not perfect. But you can bet that he understands the 'I'; he lived it for three months. It doesn't take long to kill a lifetime career, does it? It probably felt a lot longer for him as he lived through it.

However many other experts there were alongside him, however many senior colleagues might have taken decisions which led to the spill, whatever the role of the company actually operating the rig for BP – none of that mattered. He was the lightning rod. When stuff happens on your watch, make no mistake about it – it is you who must take it on the chin. His quotation shows that he gets it. For BP to move on, he had to stop being its public face. And there's no point in whining about its unfairness – it's just the way the story goes.

It could have been you

It's easy to be an armchair commentator and to join in the general fun of making fun of Tony. When other leaders are asked for their reactions, they express more empathy. Hayward took it on the chin. He didn't cling to power or complain. He could see that his leadership was incompatible with a sound future for BP, so he got out of the way. He did the right thing.

A final thought

There has been a lot of talk about self-sacrifice in this chapter, but CEOs are just humans, they are not saints. They are nonconformists who dare to do what most of us disdain to consider.[67] So it is fair to say that it doesn't feel like self-sacrifice to the leader in the job – in fact, it doesn't even feel that big a deal. As Jacko Maree says, you love the enterprise as much as your family. Just as the head of the family will represent the family and safeguard the family at all costs, so will the leader with the enterprise. It feels natural.

As one CEO put it, 'On my best day I am the company. Whether I have a good day or not, every action and inaction reflects the company, as well as changes the company.' Leadership at this level is about building a healthy, sustainable organisation. This is a big shift from performing against business results, or personal targets. Can you put the organisation ahead of your own needs? Can you see the whole enterprise and care more for the sum of the parts than for the individual parts? Can you be 'I' and 'we' all at the same time?

Unless you look out for the whole enterprise, then you will lack the objectivity to take the tough decisions. This could lead to under-performance, or sticking too long with an old strategy, or failing to keep up with change.

How far has this chapter taken you in the way you think? If you are still fighting for your corner and your personal results, you are a way from thinking like a leader. Can you look beyond this and instead aspire to what is best for the enterprise as a whole?

Developing *I am the enterprise* thinking: self assessment

Try this simple self assessment to see how close you are to thinking *I am the enterprise*.

▌ Do you have the energy it takes for sustained self-management? Are you objective enough to analyse the situation and dispassionate enough to bring to the situation what it needs? Are you always on?

▌ Can you live what the enterprise stands for? Are you obsessive about its aspirations? Do you take its goals as your own? Can you selflessly bring what the enterprise needs? Do you love the place? Can you become the place?

▌ Do you understand that, although you love the enterprise, it is not yours to control? That you can represent it, and shape it, but only at the edges? Can you accept the responsibility of the 'I' in leadership? Can you acknowledge the team that supports you, but understand that you can't hide behind them?

▌ If you are coming into the organisation from outside, can you land well? Can you imbibe the enterprise DNA so that it doesn't reject you as a foreign body? Can you love the organisation so that it loves you back? Can you live its values? Are you the enterprise?

▌ If something goes wrong, are you prepared to take it on the chin? Can you step forward and accept the responsibility? Will you step down from your job if it will make your organisation a better place, or be better placed to survive, however unfair it may feel?

chapter

7

Keep on developing

O ne of the most interesting aspects of the interviews was how the five ways of thinking rang true with all these leaders. From east to west and whether male or female, they got it really fast. The majority of them said that they had adopted at least four of these five ways of thinking. They readily identified areas that were soft spots for them – areas where they didn't believe that their thinking was sufficiently evolved. And, without being asked, they started talking about how to develop further in these areas. They saw the five as an holistic, interdependent system.

These very powerful and successful leaders were humble in the interviews. They had not fallen into the myth of infallibility and found the conversation stimulating. They appreciated a concise description of what distinguishes them and also found it a helpful way of thinking about their own next steps in development. These ways of thinking are not easy. Yet it was striking that these leaders were relaxed and accepting of them. Some felt more natural than others, depending upon the individual, yet holding them felt straightforward; it didn't require effort or tension. But neither did their relaxed embrace of these ways of thinking bring complacency. They remained restless with the status quo and endlessly curious about change and improvement. Their learning journey is not yet over.

these leaders love their jobs

Most of all, these leaders love their jobs. They are passionate about what they do and they have a lot of fun doing it. So although the hours are long and the challenges daunting to most, for them this is not just a job. It's a way of life and a life they enjoy immensely. As Niall FitzGerald of Thomson Reuters said, 'Live a life. Don't just make a living.'

Bubble wrap

But there is no doubting the strangeness of that life.

Vittorio Colao, the CEO of Vodafone, puts the challenge in a nutshell: 'One of the problems of CEOs is that we risk living in a bubble – only taking British Airways, living in airport lounges and corporate boardrooms and talking only to other CEOs. My challenge is to keep learning new things in both my personal life and my business life.' [68]

challenge is to keep learning new things

Even CEOs keep learning – or risk getting out of touch with reality. The question for you in this chapter is – how do you develop these five ways of thinking?

In the previous chapters we covered the five ways in which leaders think. The leaders discussed in this book are all CEOs or chairmen/women of global organisations, that is, they carry significant responsibilities. The preceding chapters set out the thinking in some detail, illustrated with anecdotes, examples and stories that provide a variety of leadership exemplars.

As we listen to the leaders interviewed for this book, it is not clear when they developed these ways of thinking. Some developed them younger than others. This means that, if you are in a leadership position, but not yet running the whole show, the five ways of thinking are just as relevant for you as they are for these powerful individuals.

This chapter is different. It provides advice and guidance on how to assess where you stand with these ways of thinking. Remember, they are not personality or trait based. They are the common underpinning to a wide range of actions and decisions, highly customised by each leader's personal style.

The you in unique

Your journey too will be unique, driven by your individuality. You are not constrained by your personality. And your behaviour is secondary, partly driven by how you think. For example, if you think *no safety net*, we will see you taking the initiative and pushing forward into unknown areas, with or without permission from others. If you don't think in this way, we are unlikely to see such willingness to act without instruction.

The most important next step in your development is to assess yourself on how you think now.

Taking your next step

The question is, how can you develop these five ways of thinking? There are three ways in which you can develop: you can change your way of thinking directly; you can get a coach; you can supersize it – take on a big leadership assignment and get your boss to support you. These are not dependent steps, but actions that can be taken in isolation or parallel. These three ways are easy to describe, but they all require a sophisticated level of self awareness, determination and hard work. It's just as Malcolm Gladwell explains in his book *The Tipping Point* – little things can make a big difference.[69]

You can do it with sufficient determination and practice. But to start, you need to have the fundamental desire to do so. Leaders grow into the role because they really want to be in charge. It's the absolute basic for getting ahead. It's the same with how you think.

> leaders grow into the role because they really want to be in charge

The first question you have to address is: do you really want to be a leader?

There's a moment in every leadership classroom session when I ask this question. Bear in mind that the class contains people who have given up time, energy and money to be there. So you'd expect the answer would be an unequivocal 'yes'. It never is. Typically, 20 to 30 per cent are hesitant – it's as if they are auditing the role to see if they believe that they can take it on. And I don't blame them. You can see from the stories told in this book that it's hard (but enjoyable) work.

So be sincere when you ask yourself these questions. Do you really want to change? Can you?

Lucid development

The first method of development is to change your way of thinking directly, as an effort of will. You can achieve that through exposure to the five ways of thinking that this book provides. It's a bit like going on a diet, or deciding to exercise more, once the health benefits have been explained.

So the first, and most fundamental, step in your development is self insight. Dominique Fournier, the CEO of Infineum, says that the French word 'lucide' captures this exactly – meaning that you have the capacity to see yourself as clearly as possible. You don't need to share what you know, unless you want to – but you should acknowledge it to yourself.

However, the advice to apply self insight, like a lot of leadership advice, has tended to focus on behaviour. In that context, self insight means that you should understand how you are seen by others. In many situations, a good way to do this is to undertake a 360 degree feedback process. This allows you to get a report on how you are seen by others – direct reports, peers, bosses and customers. But that approach won't work here.

> a 360 degree feedback process won't
> work here

Look inside

It won't work because the way you think is something that only you can know, as with motivation. It's pointless to look outside yourself and ask someone else for advice on what motivates you; this knowledge can only come from within. It's the same with the way you think, so this requires a process of reflection. It requires focus and honesty.

In Appendix 1 you will find an overview of the five ways of thinking in a simple table. In Appendix 2, for convenience, I have brought together the self assessment questions from the main chapters so that you can use them to guide your reflection. Be honest with yourself. Take real situations in your life and work them through to find examples of occasions when you can say that you acted or decided in a certain way, either because you did, or you didn't, think in these ways. If you find it hard to reflect on your own, ask a trusted friend or colleague to help you to think it through.

Just understanding these five ways of thinking can be a spur to change. But only if you really want to change.

A survey of the available psychometric instruments on the market shows that none of them captures these five ways of thinking.[70] My publisher, a wise and far-sighted individual, said, you know what, as there is nothing on the market, could we include something in the book? So we put together this self assessment. It's the best approach available to you.

Get a coach

Another approach to development is to find a good advisor or coach, who can help you to think through how you will make the necessary changes. This is not as straightforward as it sounds, although it can support you in self-reflection. Many executives have coaches, but it would be a mistake to think that coaching is some kind of silver bullet that will guarantee change. A lot of money is invested in coaching that fails to deliver on its promises. It is not enough to find a well-qualified coach. This is not the issue. The question you need to grapple with is whether you can respond well to the process.

So before you take a step in this direction, think about these four aspects.

Ready or not?

First, are you ready to be challenged? It can be difficult to hear views that are different to your own in something as personal as how you think about your role. It can be hard to contemplate an alternative way of thinking. This is especially true when you are successful. If you have a trusted formula and approach that has allowed you to make good progress in your career, it can be difficult to consider other options. This is just the listening part of being coached, but many fall at this first hurdle. The person being coached can hear what is being said, but they don't really believe it. Are you really ready to listen to challenges to the way you operate?

are you ready to be challenged?

The second step is to gain insight, deeper than you could through a self-reflection process. You should expect a coach to probe and dig. This is not psychoanalysis, so the probing should not feel psychologically intrusive, or stray into conversation about, say, your relationship with your parents. However, you should expect the coach to push hard, but gently. They should persist until you are sure that the way you claim to think is the same as the way you actually think. This should not be a quick and superficial analysis. Expect some push. Can you take it?

Learning to unlearn

The third aspect of being coached is to be ready to unlearn something. Of course, part of the coaching conversation should be about affirmation – encouraging you to retain the parts of your repertoire that continue to work well for you. But to move on, part of the conversation should also be about unlearning – leaving behind something that has quite possibly been part of your success formula so far, but won't get you where you need to be. It's like throwing away a much-loved shirt – you know it's a bit frayed and old-fashioned, but it takes a strong will to throw it into the bin. And, old habits are even harder to let go of than favourite old shirts.

The fourth and final step is to learn something really new. It takes time to embed new approaches and a quick fix would be exactly that. It might happen quickly, but it could fail to stick. It would certainly not be robust enough to support you as you need. With your coach's support, you will need to commit to practice and to report back to him or her, so that both of you can set and measure progress against targets.

Expect this whole process to take six months. After that, you should have made enough progress to go it alone. If you haven't, it's probably time to move on to something else.

Supersize it

The third method of development is to take on a big leadership assignment.[71] There are many studies on how adults learn and develop best and most conclude a rough 70/20/10 rule. (It is a 'rough' rule, in that the percentages vary somewhat in different research studies.) The '70' here represents the 70 per cent of development that takes place on the job – so it should be a challenging assignment; 20 per cent comes from learning from others, principally the boss; and 10 per cent from attending a development programme.

Leaders generally develop best from 'stretch' or challenging assignments, given to them as young as possible.

So a good way for you to develop these five ways of thinking is to step forward and volunteer for an assignment that will challenge you and through which you can develop. But there is a difference between taking on a job and learning from a job. Niall FitzGerald is a big believer in getting out of your comfort zone and learning through failure. He says 'I am much more shaped by things I get wrong' – because we tend to accept our successes, but dissect our failures. By reflecting on what happened, we can learn.

> volunteer for an assignment that will challenge you and through which you can develop

If you fail on the job, it is a human tendency to want to avoid the bad experience again (but see the section 'A learning mindset' below). It runs the risk of being a non-learning experience, if you convince yourself that you can't do it and so don't try again. The trick is to understand what happened and to be better armed to face a similar experience next time. Don't start with failure in mind, but don't shy away from it by staying in the safe zone either.

It's likely to have a more positive outcome if your boss (the next 20 per cent of learning opportunity) could support you. We know that it is possible to build a new way of thinking through positive reinforcement and practice.[72] The key word here is 'positive' – so try to see failure as a good outcome, rather than something to be avoided. It means you are trying hard and stretching beyond your current level of capability.

An example

Let's work through an example. Suppose that, like Jacko Maree, you have a mathematical background. You have assessed yourself against the five ways of thinking and decided that your Achilles' heel is *comfortable in discomfort*. You are conscious that you push for a decision, because you are not so comfortable with uncertainty; you are more confident in decisions where you have been able to gather adequate data. You are not sure whether you can change without support and so you have engaged a coach.

As the coach works through the five ways of thinking with you, you realise that you rely on data as the major basis for decision-making because you don't trust your own instinct. You are not sure you always know the right thing to do (*solid core*) and so you prefer to gather more information and delay the decision. Through conversation, your coach helps you to understand that your boss is getting impatient with this approach and sees you as somewhat 'stuck'.

Having reviewed the situation, you decide that it is important for your career to become more comfortable with your own decision-making instinct. You have applied for an opportunity working for your organisation in Abu Dhabi, where you know that, culturally, it is not always possible to move from 'A' to 'B' in a straight line. Decisions based purely on analysis will not be effective in a relationship-based culture, where insight into others and social instinct play a larger role. During this assignment, you intend to keep in touch with your coach to discuss your development and assess how your thinking is developing. Your boss wants you to do well and has also signed up to support you.

In this example, the young leader has decided to adopt several parallel approaches to development, in order to have a consistent and integrated path forwards. It would have been possible to choose one or two. But a combination can be more powerful.

Developing in adversity

John Wooden, revered sports coach and inspirational writer, said: 'Adversity is the state in which man most easily becomes acquainted with himself, being especially free of admirers then.'[73] Sometimes the events that shift our thinking are unplanned and unexpected. Sometimes you may face adversity, in either your professional or your personal life. It takes more resilience to learn from failure, or adversity, but such life events are great platforms for learning, even if painful. In fact, some research specifically refers to the positive impact that adversity, for example loss or illness, can have in developing leaders.[74] So if you fail, take heart. Dissect the experience and learn. Leaders pick themselves up and try again.

> if you fail, take heart

Don't skip school

Don't overlook the 10 per cent of learning that can be gained on development programmes either. Choose one that is tailored to your specific needs. For example, to develop *no safety net* thinking, a programme on strategic agility might be helpful. And it's not just about the programme content, it's also about how the content is delivered.

Adult learning methods are best focused on practice, because experienced adults learn well through action – and experience. Experiential learning means that, as a participant, you will be much more involved than with the usual lecture format used to educate students. For example, imagine learning questioning skills through role-playing a doctor trying to elicit and diagnose a patient's illness. Or developing advocacy skills through role-playing a lawyer in a courtroom trial, either defending or prosecuting your company against a relevant charge (for example, this company stands accused of failing to develop its leadership talent).

> adult learning methods are best focused on practice

Because learners become immersed in the activity, their experience feels more like real life (and less like classroom learning, which can feel divorced from reality for many executives – too theoretical).

All revved up

Imagine this scene. A group of executives is learning how to accelerate the performance of a team through being the pit crew team on a racing car. The racing car (a real one) has just roared to a stop in the pits and the team is trying to beat its own time for changing all four tyres. One executive, who has been puzzling over feedback from work that he is not a good team member, hears his phone ring and abruptly steps aside to take the call. In the middle of the record attempt. The very real feedback he received from the team showed him exactly why people at work considered him a poor team player.

So the advice here is to look for a development programme that has the right content and also the right learning experience. It will be easier for you to apply what you have learnt back at work if you have the opportunity to practise first, in a 'safe' environment, away from work.

Another growth spurt

At the top, everyone thinks that you have made it. And in one way you have, because you have been successful in gaining the ultimate prize – the boss's job.

But, as conversations with these enormously successful people demonstrate, the journey doesn't stop there. Dominique Fournier of Infineum explains how it works for him. 'My engine for growth is that I acknowledge to myself that I don't know everything and can still learn. People who are very intelligent do not always listen, because they believe that they should know more than others.' As we discussed earlier, being above average in intelligence is one of the reasons a leader gets the job in the first place. Be careful this doesn't stop you listening and continuing to learn.

> even CEOs still develop and grow

Once you cross that threshold into the executive suite, there is still further to go. Let's pause and think about the idea that even CEOs still develop and grow. Shouldn't getting the CEO position mean that you have made it? Haven't you reached the pinnacle of corporate endeavour?

A story here may help to illustrate the continuing development journey for a leader.

Back to front

Let's go back to the leader we met in Chapter 1. It's 2003. Dennis Nally has been Chairman and Senior Partner of PricewaterhouseCoopers LLP, the PwC United States firm, since 2002. Under his leadership, once every month for 18 months, he and his executive team meet at a giant conference centre in New Jersey, USA. They host up to 150 senior partners at a time. The agenda? To motivate and energise the entire US practice.

Dennis always looks calm. As he leads sessions from the stage, or walks the halls, or hosts dinner, there is always a smile close to his lips and a measured expression in his eyes. This is certainly a huge investment of his time and it's important to him.

It's the midweek evening session and we have a private room. The plan is for Dennis to give a short talk before dinner, reminding the partners why they are gathered together and where the firm is headed next. A leadership moment and a strategic look ahead. One of the longer-serving partners is boisterous. She's missed the point. In her mind, the evening is for relaxing with colleagues and having a few laughs. She's running from group to group, starting a few games and generally turning it into a bit of a party. No harm in that, the networking and relaxation are an important part of building camaraderie across nearly 2,000 partners. But it's getting in the way of the serious message that Dennis wants to deliver. He watches and makes no move to intervene. He hasn't been in the job that long.

Act like the CEO

The team swings into action, rallies around him and gets things back on track. The games are halted, the partners seated and Dennis takes control of the microphone. A few key messages and dinner starts. As I walk past him he smiles and says 'Thanks, Mom'. (It was a nice compliment.)

In March 2009, Dennis was elected Chairman of the PwC International Network for a four-year term – effectively global chairman. It's hard to imagine him missing a beat like that today (or, indeed, calling me 'Mom'). He grew into the role and then grew some more, to the role of chairman. Talking to him today, it's clear that even this is unlikely to be the end of his development and success as a leader. He loves his work. He always wants to do more, to be better.

What's the point of this story? It's to say that even the smartest and the best leaders continue to grow. They never stop. And these five ways of thinking can help you to keep developing. In the interviews, the leaders practised three to five of these ways of thinking. They aspired to all five. They knew they had further to go.

> even the smartest and the best leaders
> continue to grow

Start young

One of the best ways to develop leaders is to give talented people a lot of responsibility, as young as possible. So when should you start thinking like a leader? The same advice seems to fit – as young as possible. In the interviews, at some point the leader would say something like 'I don't know where it comes from. I've always thought this way.'

Let's take one young leader's story and see what it tells us. This is a true, but anonymous, story.

Chris is young and a leader. He is nearer the start of his journey than the end of it, both at work and at home, where he is the father of very young children. He is already successful and is one of a handful of young executives being hand groomed by the CEO as part of his succession plan. As part of their development, this group is being asked to undertake strategic projects to move the company forward. Chris is bright and has the exceptional ability to reflect on events with an open and learning mind. He also does it out loud, so it's easy to follow his thinking.

One strategic aim for his company is to become more collaborative as a culture, to learn more from each other and to share and adopt best practices. Chris suggested to his colleagues that they adopt just one business project and collaborate on it, rather than tackle several projects in small groups. In this way, they would be able to deliver business results and at the same time symbolise the more collaborative culture that they aim to build. His idea was adopted enthusiastically and his colleagues also appointed him to lead them in the project.

This took Chris by surprise, and he was reluctant at first. He wasn't sure he wanted to lead – he saw it as more work, rather than as a vote of confidence from his peers. But he did believe that the whole group acting as one team was symbolically important for the company, so he accepted the role.

What can we learn from Chris? He is talented enough to be part of the CEO's chosen group and he has also been nominated as a leader by his peers (and peers are often your hardest critics). What is the extra ingredient?

Chris thinks like a leader. The way his mind works is just different. He is not necessarily more creative, more of a right-brain thinker or a more lateral thinker. But in this story, he has demonstrated at least one of the five distinctive ways in which a leader thinks. In this case, he is thinking *I am the enterprise*. He is putting the enterprise before his own needs.

A learning mindset

This book strongly supports the notion that your mindset determines your actions. That is, the way you see the world will determine how you react to it.

So, sometimes, personal development starts with understanding your own mindset. The reasoning is that if your mental attitude is fixed, it's unlikely that your approach will be flexible. Unless you change your mind, you won't change your outlook, opinion or behaviour.

A growth mindset

There is such a thing as a learning mindset.[75] Research looked at how people from young schoolchildren to professional footballers learn and develop. It concluded that if the learner has a growth mindset and believes that she or he can improve their abilities and accomplishments through purposeful effort, the student excels – both at studies and in life.

The reasoning goes something like this. I believe that I can improve and so I have a desire to learn and a tendency to embrace challenges. I continue to persist, even in the face of setbacks, and believe that putting in effort will make me better. I take risks and see mistakes as a chance to learn. I can learn from criticism. I find lessons and inspiration in the achievements of others and so I continue to grow.

> I take risks and see mistakes as a chance
> to learn

The author, Carol Dweck, a pychologist from Stanford University, contrasts this with people with a fixed mindset, those who believe that their intrinsic worth is set and so they stagnate. They follow almost the opposite reasoning. I believe that I am as smart as I can be, so I am always trying to safeguard my reputation. I avoid challenges; give up easily in the face of obstacles; think that effort is useless; avoid constructive criticism; am jealous of the success of others; and end up failing to maximise my potential.

Mindset defined as a closed or open approach to learning makes good sense. Dweck also mentions the role that effort plays in learning and the impact of believing that sustained effort will get you where you want to go. Those with a fixed mindset are prone to blame everything and everyone except themselves for their own failings. They can't admit that talent isn't that important and that personal weak performance can be traced back directly to their own lack of effort. Achievement is not effortless, it takes hard work to learn and improve.

Back to Bing

This story also takes us back to Bing Nursery School at Stanford, mentioned in Chapter 5 in the story of marshmallows and delayed gratification. Today, Dweck is working at Bing, trying to instil into 4-year-olds a belief in their capacity to be 'good' – to learn how to do better – even though they may have been 'bad' in the past. She is teaching them how to learn.

What did I learn?

This is an author's footnote. I wasn't sure where to put it, but in the chapter about learning seems to make most sense. After 25 years in the business of leadership development, I am still learning. There were some surprises for me in this research that I'd like to share.

The first surprise was how closely the leaders I talked to identify with their organisations. I talk about it in Chapter 6 as being a symbiotic relationship – the leader relies on the organisation for survival and vice versa. I had expected to find good role models. I had not expected to find devotees who give whatever it takes. There is huge commitment to the bigger ideal of sustainability, heightened levels of responsibility and emotion in this job.

The second was how cheerful and optimistic they are. I remember years ago writing a leadership skills journal for MBAs and including a cartoon. The character is floating in a spacesuit, with amazing views of the earth from space, close to the glowing moon and surrounded by stars. Magical. The speech bubble coming out of the spacesuit is 'so what?' The point I was making is that leaders are enthusiastic cheerleaders, not cynics. I didn't realise how innate this is. Whether they are 'always on' and managing their bad days, or just really upbeat, makes no difference on the receiving end. It is uplifting. ▶

The last was how humble these powerful leaders are. When Jim Collins[76] described leadership humility, he was looking specifically at leaders of out-performing companies. My sample was more random – I tried to get a lot of diversity into the sample (not diversity in terms of company performance – the leaders were all running large, successful organisations – but diversity of personality, ethnicity, gender, style and background). So I was surprised by how self-deprecating and welcoming they are, irrespective of the differences among them. They spend a lot of time thinking about who they are and what they should do for the common good. They took the interview as another opportunity to reflect and learn.

My sincere hope is that the ideas in this book help you reflect and learn as a leader too.

Endnotes

1 This is a view that was shared by one of the greatest headhunters of his time, John Viney, CEO, Zygos Partnership and former Head of Europe, Heidrick & Struggles. John, astrophysicist and musician turned headhunter, was a prodigious talent whose forensic interviewing skills differentiated between the good and the great when he was looking for CEOs or board-level executives. John died in 2009.

2 *Leading Change,* John P. Kotter, Harvard Business School Press, 1996.

3 'Alico to split from AIG', David Masters, *Insurance Daily,* 17 July 2009.

4 *Nelson Mandela: Robben Island to Rainbow Nation (Inspirations),* Marian Pallister and Rosemary Goring, Argyll, 2010.

5 *CEO: The Low-Down on the Top Job,* Kevin Kelly, Prentice Hall, 2008.

6 Chris Cappy spent many years working at GE's famous leadership development centre in Crotonville, New York. One of his best insights is when he talks about 50 reasons people find to avoid change, everything from 'it's against tradition' to 'I'm all for it, but ...'.

7 *Ford Tough: Bill Ford and the Battle to Rebuild America's Automaker,* David Magee, John Wiley & Sons, 2005.

8 www.autoblog.com, 14 April 2010.

9 Julia Kollewe, 'RBS chief Sir Fred rejects charge of "megalomania"', *The Independent,* 5 August 2005.

10 Alex Brummer, 'PROFILE: Fred the Shred fails his final fitness test', *Daily Mail,* 13 October 2008.

11 Gary Latham, an old friend, loves to say this.

12 'C-Suite Strategies: Making big drugs during troubled times', Geoff Colvin, *Fortune,* 9 July 2009, interview with Amgen CEO Kevin Sharer (answering 'Why are investors and the industry so interested in denosumab?').

13 *Wall Street Journal*, 6 July 2010, quoting a study by Spencer Stuart.

14 *Straight Talk about Mental Tests,* Arthur Jensen, Free Press, 1981.

15 'Chinese bank stake paying off for Standard', Sure Kamhunga, Business Day South Africa Report, 31 August 2010.

16 Commissioner Luis A. Aguilar of the US Securities and Exchange Commission gave a speech to the SAIS Center for Transatlantic Relations in Washington DC on 16 September 2010. He talked about the persistent lack of diversity at the top of organisations, and particularly the lack of gender diversity.

17 *Decision Analysis for Management Judgment,* Paul Goodwin and George Wright, John Wiley & Sons, 2009.

18 *Relax, It's Only Uncertainty,* Philip Hodgson and Randall P. White, FT Prentice Hall, 2001.

19 *Judgment: How Winning Leaders Make Great Calls,* Noel M. Tichy and Warren G. Bennis, Portfolio Books, 2007.

20 The arabesque is a classic pose in ballet in which the dancer stands on one leg, straight or bent, with the other leg raised behind, fully extended. In business vernacular, it refers to a sideways move, so that incompetent managers get lateral moves with a longer job title, to save face (*The Peter Principle: Why Things Always Go Wrong,* Laurence J. Peter and Raymond Hull, William Morrow, 1969: a Dilbert before his time and worth reading). In academic terms, it's when a subject becomes so academic that its relevance to the real world disappears. Here, the meaning is simply that of a surprise move.

21 *Redefining the Corporation: Stakeholder Management and Organizational Wealth,* James E. Post, Lee E. Preston and Sybille Sachs, Stanford Business Books, 2002.

22 The *Oxford Dictionary of Psychology* defines 'imposter phenomenon' as 'a subjective experience of phoniness in people who believe that they are not intelligent, capable or creative despite evidence of high achievement, and who are highly motivated to achieve but live in perpetual fear of being "found out" or exposed as frauds'.

23 *Managing Up* (Harvard Pocket Mentor), Harvard Business School, 2008.

24 *The King of Sunlight: How William Lever Cleaned Up The World,* Adam Macqueen, Corgi, 2005.

25 *William Hesketh Lever: Port Sunlight and Port Fishlight,* Development Trust Association, 2007.

26 *The Rise of Corporate Global Power,* Sarah Anderson and John Cavanagh, Institute for Policy Studies, 2000. Comparison between the size of a company and that of a country is based on corporate sales and country GDPs.

27 *Challenger,* director Glenn Jordan, February 1990. The film profiles astronauts, crew and civilians involved in the 28 January 1986 Challenger launch, which exploded on takeoff. The film revolves around arguments about the o-rings that were ultimately blamed for the explosion.

28 *Good Value: Reflections on Money, Morality and an Uncertain World,* Stephen Green, Allen Lane, 2009.

29 The *Telegraph* newspaper on 11 September 2010 set out a more cynical view. The government has insufficient backing for their 'big idea' to split up the banks, in case they abandon the UK in favour of geographies without such restrictions. Stephen Green's banking expertise will help him to be creative and offer alternatives – he thinks that while banks shouldn't be too big to fail, at the same time they need to be big enough to cope.

30 *How We Decide,* Jonah Lehrer, Houghton Mifflin Harcourt, 2009. In this book, Lehrer describes how humans need both their rational and emotional brains to combine to reach a decision. In fact, without the emotional part of our brain, reason would not exist at all – it is the final arbiter. Lehrer also wrote *Proust was a Neuroscientist.*

31 *Mandela: The Authorised Portrait,* PQ Blackwell, 2006.

32 Ibid.

33 'HSBC in bid to raise £12.5bn', Russell Lynch, *The Independent,* 2 March 2009.

34 *America, Russia, and the Cold War, 1945–2006,* Walter LaFeber, McGraw-Hill, 2008.

35 'Likeableness ratings of SST personality trait words', N.H. Anderson, *Journal of Personality and Social Psychology,* 1968, pp. 272–9.

36 'Not Pollyannas: Higher generalized trust predicts lie detection ability', Nancy Carter and J. Mark Weber, *Social Psychological & Personality Science*, vol. 1, no. 3, 2010, pp. 274–9.

37 *Good to Great: Why Some Companies Make the Leap … and Others Don't*, Jim Collins, Random House Business, 2001.

38 *Enron: The Rise and Fall*, Loren Fox, John Wiley & Sons, 2003.

39 *The Smartest Guys in the Room: The Amazing Rise and Scandalous Fall of Enron*, Bethany McLean and Peter Elkind, Portfolio, 2004.

40 *Who Says Elephants Can't Dance? Inside IBM's Historic Turnaround*, Louis Gerstner, HarperBusiness, 2002.

41 'Gerstner: Changing culture at IBM', Martha Lagace, *HBS Working Knowledge*, 9 December 2002.

42 *The birth of Nokia – Nokia's first century*, Nokia Corporation.

43 'Molecular structure of nucleic acids: A structure for deoxyribose nucleic acid', James D. Watson and Frances Crick, *Nature*, 171, 25 April 1953, pp. 737–8.

44 *Organizational Culture and Leadership*, Edgar Schein, Jossey-Bass, 1992.

45 'The ten best mass insults', Simon Rice, *The Independent,* 9 October 2009. Brian Clough died in 2004 at the age of 69.

46 'Occupying powers', Dennis Potter, *The Guardian*, 28 August 1993.

47 'Is the Internet making us stupid?', Nicholas Carr, *The Times*, 14 August 2010.

48 *The Shallows: What the Internet Is Doing to Our Brains*, Nicholas Carr, W. W. Norton, 2010.

49 *Emotional Intelligence: Why It Can Matter More than IQ*, Daniel Goleman, Bloomsbury, 1996.

50 *Frederick W. Taylor and the Rise of Scientific Management,* Daniel Nelson, University of Wisconsin Press, 1980.

51 The Hawthorne Studies were carried out at the Western Electric Hawthorne Works in Chicago by the Harvard Professor Elton Mayo, between 1927 and 1932. They built on earlier experiments looking at the effect of lighting levels on productivity. Changes to working conditions were made and reversed, yet productivity continued to

rise in the group of six female workers selected for the study. The conclusions were revolutionary at the time, as it became apparent that feedback and the perception of being a self-managed work team caused the rises in productivity. The impact of how people feel about the job started to become as important as how the job is organised.

52 *International Dimensions of Organizational Behavior,* Nancy J. Adler, South-Western College Publishing, 1997.

53 'Tech's all-time top 25 flops: 6. Carly Fiorina', Infoworld, 21 January 2008.

54 'Eight years and $14 billion later, HP ex-chief Fiorina vindicated', Loren Steffy, *New York Times,* 14 May 2008.

55 *Tough Choices: A Memoir,* Carly Fiorina, Portfolio, 2006.

56 Spoken statement from about 1903, reported in *Harper's Monthly* in September 1932.

57 Reported statement from 1877, quoted in *From Telegraph to Light Bulb with Thomas Edison,* Deborah Hedstrom-Page, B&H, 2007.

58 *Managing Your Self: Management by Detached Involvement,* Jagdish Parikh, Blackwell, 1993.

59 London Business School, *Business Strategy Review,* Autumn 2010.

60 Ibid.

61 *Marks in Time: 125 Years of Marks & Spencer,* Helen Chislett, Weidenfeld & Nicolson, 2009.

62 Interview with Sir Stuart Rose, Chris Blackhurst, *Management Today,* 4 December 2006.

63 Ibid.

64 'Gerstner: Changing culture at IBM', Martha Lagace, *HBS Working Knowledge,* 9 December 2002.

65 In the days of the Wild West in the USA, poker players placed a knife with a buckhorn handle in front of the dealer; if you chose not to deal, you 'passed the buck'.

66 Tony Hayward quoted on Channel Four News, 27 July 2010.

67 *Drive: Leadership in Business and Beyond,* John Viney, Bloomsbury, 1999, p. 24.

68 London Business School, *Business Strategy Review*, Autumn 2010.

69 *The Tipping Point: How Little Things Can Make a Big Difference,* Malcolm Gladwell, Little, Brown, 2000.

70 Psychometric and other instruments surveyed where some (limited) measurement of the five ways of thinking were found included the Hogan Personality Inventory (weakest), the Leadership Versatility Index (Kaiser and Kaplan), the Global Personality Inventory (strongest) and the NEO Personality Inventory Revised.

71 *The Lessons of Experience: How Successful Executives Develop on the Job,* Morgan W. McCall, Michael M. Lombardo and Ann M. Morrison 1988.

72 *Becoming the Evidence Based Manager,* Gary P. Latham, Davies-Black, 2009.

73 www.brainyquote.com/quotes/authors/j/john_wooden.html, 17 December 2010.

74 'Managers and leaders: Are they different?', Abraham Zaleznik, *Harvard Business Review,* 1977.

75 *Mindset. The New Psychology of Success,* Carol S. Dweck, Random House, 2006.

76 *Good to Great: Why Some Companies Make the Leap ... and Others Don't,* Jim Collins, Random House Business, 2001.

Further reading

While books with 'leader' or 'leadership' in the title offer great advice, we shouldn't confine ourselves to the leadership literature. To do so risks overlooking ideas that don't come under this banner, but nonetheless offer tremendous insight to existing and aspiring leaders.

Here is a short reading list you may find useful.

Winning 'em Over: A New Model for Managing in the Age of Persuasion, Jay Conger, Simon & Schuster, 1998. Getting stuff done in a complex world requires excellent influencing skills, even for the leader. This book stands out and was an early advocate for storytelling as a way to build emotional connections as a leader.

Emotional Intelligence: Why It Can Matter More Than IQ, Daniel Goleman, Bloomsbury, 1996. This book reminded us all of the power of emotions, the need to be in command of our own as a leader and to empathise with those of others.

Predictably Irrational: The Hidden Forces that Shape Our Decisions, Dan Ariely, HarperCollins, 2008. The fight between economists and psychologists has always been about the predictability or irrationality of the human species. This book brilliantly ties both together and helps any leaders to understand followers better.

Corps Business: The 30 Management Principles of the U.S. Marines, David H. Freedman, HarperBusiness, 2000. As any leader will tell you, managing the business intangibles is as important as managing the business. This book gives real insight into how to understand culture, motivation and other important intangibles.

Drive: Leadership in Business and Beyond, John Viney, Bloomsbury, 1999. John was one of the most gifted headhunters of his generation until his untimely death in 2009. The chapter 'Why Leaders Fail' is a must-read.

The Lexus and the Olive Tree, Thomas L. Friedman, Anchor Books, 2000. This explains globalisation, the backdrop to how we all work today.

In Over Our Heads: The Mental Demands of Modern Life, Robert Kegan, Harvard University Press, 1994. A striking aspect to all the leaders interviewed for this book is that they are at peace with the world and themselves. Both this book and the next in the list help us to overcome the ways in which we can get in the way of our own leadership success.

Why Zebras Don't Get Ulcers: An Updated Guide to Stress, Stress-Related Diseases and Coping, Robert M. Sapolsky, W. H. Freeman, 1998. As above.

The Trusted Advisor, David H. Maister, Charles H. Green and Robert M. Galford, Free Press, 2000. Again, a debate between economists and psychologists on how we build trust with others. This book squares the circle and offers a simple recipe for building long-lasting trust.

Five Minds for the Future, Howard Gardner, Harvard Business School Press, 2006. This talented author sets out five new ways of thinking and learning to help us to cope with a globalised world.

How We Decide, Jonah Lehrer, Houghton Mifflin Harcourt, 2009. Lehrer uses stories to describe good and poor decisions, along with advice on when to rely on emotion, when to use logic and when to just mull it over in the mind. Brilliant to understand the pivotal role of emotion in taking a logical decision.

Drive: The Surprising Truth about What Motivates Us, Daniel H. Pink, Canongate, 2010. At last a book that puts money as a motivator into its (unhelpful) place. The YouTube clip by the Royal Society of Arts is great if you prefer the 10-minute version.

'The five minds of a manager', Jonathan Gosling and Henry Mintzberg, *Harvard Business Review,* 1 November 2003. Following the great thinker Charles Hampden-Turner in highlighting the role of dilemmas in executive thinking, this article highlights five specific dilemmas that they believe managers face. And because good things come in fives.

Appendix 1
Overview of the five ways of thinking

The table on the following page contrasts the difference between thinking like a senior executive and thinking like the CEO. Use it to consider the way in which you think right now.

Draw a line across the page for each mindset and place a mark to represent where you are in your own thinking today. Are you closer to the senior executive or closer to the CEO way of thinking? Then use the self assessment questions which follow to guide you in developing further the way in which you think. Use them to help you think even more like a leader.

The senior executive way of thinking	Becomes this as the CEO
Move from pragmatic decision-making to leading the enterprise into uncharted territory	
I have a well developed and business-minded outlook. I understand the need to balance risk and reward and take sound decisions. I am pragmatic and make sure that I both consult and advise.	I act at the edge of uncertainty and I am willing to take decisions that move the enterprise into uncharted territory. At the point of decision, there is no-one else to look to for reassurance, I am alone. I am not waiting for permission and I am willing to lean into unknown risk. I am unafraid. **No safety net**.
Move beyond the data to making a judgement call fraught with complexity and uncertainty	
I have a huge capacity for data and synthesis; an ability to crunch data, find the flaws, and make the call now, yes or no. I take a decision and stand by it.	The complexity of the situation means that there is no right answer. Sometimes there is not enough data and I know that, despite this, the decision cannot be delayed. Sometimes I have all the data I need but I know that it's best to delay. I can live with the uncertainty and not transit it to others. **Comfortable in discomfort**.
Move from looking confident to trusting an internal compass for what makes a difference	
I appear confident and have leadership presence. People follow me because they believe in me and I can inspire confidence in them that we will go in the right direction.	An inner sense of purpose strengthens my authenticity. I have a heightened sense of integrity that is driven from within. I know where I am coming from and I can chart a direction based on this inner compass. I am grounded, calm and have a clear sense of purpose from within. **Solid core**.

Move from being absorbed by the business of the day to living in three time zones without jet lag	
I spend my time primarily fixing and growing today's business, because the analysts are unforgiving if you miss a beat on the quarterly results. I spend the rest of the time thinking about a 5–10-year horizon on the future.	It's not just about where the organisation is heading, but also about making sure that I integrate the past into the future. I capture unique elements of the enterprise heritage, so that I can help others see the bigger purpose, but I can also let the past go if it might harm the future. I can live in three time zones simultaneously to weave the enterprise story. ***On my watch***.
Move from focusing on personal business results to embodying the enterprise and its aspirations	
I am adept at getting things done and delivering results. I am happy to accept accountability. I understand how the business works and I am good at my job.	I understand not just what the enterprise does, but the core reason it exists. I embody what the enterprise stands for, I live and represent its values. I am fully committed to the enterprise and I have the energy to manage myself so that I always represent it faithfully. And if it all goes wrong, I am ready to take the blame and step down, so that the enterprise can continue to flourish. ***I am the enterprise***.

Appendix 2
Self-assessment questions

No safety net

▌ Do you understand that you are alone? Are you willing to be the one to stand up and take the difficult decision? Do you understand that you are paid to take the big risks?

▌ Have you got the courage to take the first step? Do you realise that nothing will happen until you move? Can you take the first step without thought for your personal consequences?

▌ Can you ensure you won't get so far ahead that you look like the enemy? Can you take people with you? Will they trust you?

▌ Can you keep a good healthy dose of self doubt? Can you keep listening despite the tumult you create by moving the enterprise? Can you keep an open mind while looking confident to others?

▌ Are you brave enough to fail? Do you have the courage to accept the stigma of failure? Are you resilient enough to try again?

Comfortable in discomfort

▌ Can you live with grey, rather than the immediate certainty of a black and white answer? Can you call it even when the data isn't there?

▌ Can you learn to love ambiguity? Can you move forward effectively in ambiguity and not become frozen by uncertainty or driven to repeat earlier routines?

▌ Can you resist the temptation to close down the debate and decide? Can you hold back and stop yourself from driving to a conclusion? Can you create and hold the tension to reach a better answer?

▌Can you retain the power of surprise? Can you hold your mind open to new ideas and change direction in a way that creates more value?

▌Can you hold up and speak to an exciting future vision, even if the way forward isn't crystal clear? Can you hold your own vulnerability in check so that others have the courage to follow you?

Solid core

▌Do you have an inner compass? Do you live your life according to clear personal values? Do you have irreproachable integrity?

▌Do you share this inner compass with others? Do people know what these values are? Can they see how these values guide your decisions and actions?

▌Do you have an internal sense of the right thing to do? Can you rise above the politics? Can you demonstrate your internal conviction in ways that others can see?

▌Are you authentic? Do you know that this is not just the same as being yourself?

▌Do you show humility? At the same time, can you retain a strong ego? Do you have the courage not to surround yourself with cronies? Can you keep open to others' real opinion of you?

On my watch

▌Do you consciously think about three time zones? Do you respect and integrate the history of the organisation? When you move to change business, do people follow you because they know that you respect the past that they created?

▌Can you deal with the tyranny of the present, without being enslaved to it? Can you avoid getting trapped into constant crisis management? Can you live without the executive 'high' of firefighting?

- Do you spend enough time thinking about the future? Can you delay gratification and sacrifice instant reward so that you can build the future? Can you leave the path that got the organisation to where it is today and adopt a different and better route forwards?

- Can you juggle living in three time zones and not get jetlag? Can you integrate three time horizons as you tell the stories that explain the heritage of the organisation and what makes the present work well, and encourage others to join you in a different future?

- Can you think about your tenure of leadership as fleeting and temporary? Can you accept and pass the baton of leadership seamlessly, from and to the former and next generation of leaders? Do you worry less about your legacy and more about your stewardship?

I am the enterprise

- Do you have the energy it takes for sustained self-management? Are you objective enough to analyse the situation and dispassionate enough to bring to the situation what it needs? Are you always on?

- Can you live what the enterprise stands for? Are you obsessive about its aspirations? Do you take its goals as your own? Can you selflessly bring what the enterprise needs? Do you love the place? Can you become the place?

- Do you understand that, although you love the enterprise, it is not yours to control? That you can represent it, and shape it, but only at the edges? Can you accept the responsibility of the 'I' in leadership? Can you acknowledge the team that supports you, but understand that you can't hide behind them?

- If you are coming into the organisation from outside, can you land well? Can you imbibe the enterprise DNA so that it doesn't reject you as a foreign body? Can you love the organisation so that it loves you back? Can you live its values? Are you the enterprise?

▌ If something goes wrong, are you prepared to take it on the chin? Can you step forward and accept the responsibility? Will you step down from your job if it will make your organisation a better place, or be better placed to survive, however unfair it may feel?

Index

READ ON

"This is a brilliant little guide that'll help you every day. Keep it with you. I do."
Chris Pilling, Chief Executive, First Direct

Leadership
Plain and Simple

Steve Radcliffe   **FT** Prentice Hall
FINANCIAL TIMES

9780273730897

A LEADER'S GUIDE TO
INFLUENCE

MIKE BRENT AND FIONA DENT   **FT** Prentice Hall
FINANCIAL TIMES

9780273729860

'The most practical guide to leadership I've read in many a day'
Graeme Thomson, Head of Strategy, TAI Group

THE LEADERSHIP BOOK

FIRST DAYS IN THE JOB TRUSTING YOUR INSTINCTS MANAGING MEETINGS
TIME MANAGEMENT LEADING PRODUCT DEVELOPMENT MANAGING CHANGE
LEADING STRATEGY BUILDING & MANAGING RELATIONSHIPS MANAGING COSTS

MARK ANDERSON   **FT** Prentice Hall
FINANCIAL TIMES

9780273732044

HOW TO LEAD
2nd Edition

JO OWEN

9780273721505

Available now online and at all good bookstores
www.pearson-books.com

PEARSON